TRANSCEND
A NEW WAY FORWARD

WORKBOOK

**AN ISTORIA MINISTRY GROUP PROGRAM
TO DISCOVER LASTING PEACE**

CHRIS WASMAN

BRIGHTRAY
PUBLISHING

We help busy professionals write and publish their stories to distinguish themselves and their brands.

(407) 287-5700 | Winter Park, FL
info@BrightRay.com | www.BrightRay.com

ISBN: 978-1-956464-21-4

Published in the United States of America.
BrightRay Publishing 2022

TABLE OF CONTENTS

APPENDIX

INTRODUCTION

"Istoría" is the Greek translation for both of the words "story" and "history," which captures the essence of our ministry. Why the story theme?

Our whole lives are lived out and captured in the context of stories. Memories are recalled this way. Traditions are passed down this way. History is written this way. Online profiles are now created for this very purpose. Some of our favorite books, movies, and music capture our hearts by telling powerful stories. Everyone has a story to tell. The stories we tell are reflections of who we have been, who we are today, and who we will become. Telling them matters! Our passion and calling at IMG is making a positive impact on as many people as possible and changing history by helping them refine their stories.

Sadly, it seems most people are too impatient to take the time to listen to the whole story. I'm guilty of asking my own family to "give me the bullet points" at times, but a good story is one worth being retold over and over again in full. In fact, my kids will often say, "Dad, tell us the one about Uncle Brian running into the sliding glass door again," or, "Tell us about when you messed your pants as a baby on that ride at Disney World." Sometimes, the most disastrous of experiences turn into the greatest stories later down the road. For the most part now, the stories we hear are the Facebook versions with only the positive highlights. They don't show the real us.

Perhaps the real story about someone is what can be said about their deepest convictions, their character, and whether they made their story all about themselves or those around them. So, what's your story? Better yet, what would you like your story to be?

Surely there are things which you would like to edit in your story or even remove completely, given the chance. But what if God used those very things as the means for you to connect to Him and others in a much deeper way? What if those things became the start of a narrative which ended in victory? I love a good underdog or comeback story. There's something inspiring about a character who overcomes the odds to win it all, which sparks hope in me and makes me feel like if they can do it, maybe I can, too. I mean, come on—Henry Ford, Steve Jobs, Jackie Robinson… the list goes on. Everyone loves rooting for the underdog.

The similarity in all of their stories is how they seemingly had the odds stacked against them, found a way to transcend the standards imposed on them, and somehow succeeded. In every case, they were able to respond in this way because they stood for something so much bigger than themselves. Maybe it was for another person or an organization, or sometimes it was simply an ideal in which they wholeheartedly believed. The challenges, brokenness, and despair seemed to ignite something in each of them, only making them stronger and even more determined.

Would you be surprised if I told you that those stories are way more prevalent than you might think? What if I told you that you are surrounded by them and walk past them every day? What if I told you that you could have one of them? If we took the time to ask the people around us what they've battled and overcome to be here today, you would be amazed. All around you each day, there are stories of people finding victory over loss, addiction, abuse, sickness, betrayal, financial ruin, and all sorts of trauma that would blow your mind if you knew. Maybe you have one of these stories, yet many people hesitate to talk about the harder parts of the story. Why?

Well, we would have to move beyond the surface level with each other in order to get to this part of the story, which can be awkward or even scary. Additionally, it requires some work that we may not have been willing to put in before in order to be comfortable enough to talk about it. However, once you know someone's story, you develop a compassion for them with your new perspective.

All of our stories are vastly different but have intersected here, and we believe it's for a reason.

The good news is that once we discover the person we've been made to be and realize the value in every part of our unique stories, there is great peace and joy in it. Lasting peace and true joy are two things that most any person would agree to desire deeply. I've learned that the only way to truly experience these feelings is by going beyond the surface level with God and others in order to form real relationships. Most Christians would probably agree with what I've said so far with no problems. However, most of those same Christians are also still living in a cycle of unrest and anxiety like their non-believing friends. So, what is the disconnect? Why can we seemingly be moved so deeply by worship or a powerful sermon on Sunday only to find ourselves yielding to the chaos again on Monday? We manage to maintain our passion for faith for a while, but then something happens that makes us question whether any of our efforts are worth it. This is the cycle of unrest—a result of surface-level relationships and surface-level faith.

WORKBOOK DIRECTIONS

As the program proceeds, please follow along and fill in the blanks. Once completed, you can check your answers using the answer key provided at the end of the workbook.

CHAPTER 1

THE PROBLEM
AND THE SOLUTION

What is _____ faith? It was me as a child attending Catholic church each Sunday but only looking forward to stopping at the donut shop on the way home. It was me going through the motions of first communion and confirmation, serving as an altar boy, and attending youth groups but not grasping the real significance of any of it. It was me, not too many years ago, with a job and a family and a life that appeared perfect on the outside, but I had no relationship with Jesus. I walked into church on Sundays with my family, dealing out high fives to everyone who wanted one, serving on a team, and even participating in a Bible study group. So many of the interactions looked the same: "Hey man, good to see you. How are you doing? Let's get the family together sometime." Then, I'd move on to the next surface-level line with the next person. I had successfully buried all of the parts of my story that I didn't like well enough to coat the outside of my story and give the impression that I had it all together.

Eventually, I found a Christian nondenominational church that preached messages directly from the Bible, and I decided to actually give God a chance at driving. Not long after this, life dealt me a card that brought me to my knees in despair. I was forced to reconcile what I said I believed and how I would respond next. What I wanted to do and what the Christian faith asked of me were two very different responses. There would be no disguising where I stood, and I could not see a way to walk out of my faith without some supernatural takeover of sorts. Like many do, I cried out to God, "If You are really there and what the Bible says is actually true, I need You right now. In fact, I'm not strong enough to do what You're calling me towards, so You will need to drag me through this next part of life if I am even to make it." This was the beginning of the journey that led me out of my surface-level faith, and although I didn't know it at the time, this would bring me into a ministry focused on helping others realize the same.

The following years brought education, experience, and visibility into just how big the problem with surface-level Christianity was. James 1:22 would ring out in my mind as I began to see the disconnect with so many: "Do not merely listen to the word, and so deceive yourselves. Do what it says." It wasn't just the people attending church. This shallowness had even shown itself in some of the church leaders. How could this be, though? How could someone who felt called by God as a pastor or leader be living a life that did not align with what they claimed to believe? If they couldn't live out their faith, how could the rest of us?

This reality check begged the question that haunted me for so long. Do I really believe what I say I believe? Do I believe it so firmly that it changes how I live my life and how I treat other people? Would I be willing to die for my beliefs like those in the Bible, or did I casually subscribe to them when it was convenient or made me look better? Do I merely claim to be a believer, or is it evident that I am a _____? How deep does my faith run? Is this trap of surface-level faith what Jesus warns us about when he mentions the "lukewarm" in Revelation 3:15-16?

Around this same time, I came across something in my reading that scared me about the potential scope of this surface-level faith problem. I read that Billy Graham once stated he believed 85% of the millions of people he reached through his years in ministry would not make it to heaven. Could this be true? W. A. Criswell also said, "I would be surprised to see even 25% of my church members in heaven." Well, Jesus made a similarly shocking statement during His Sermon on the Mount, as recorded by Matthew:

"Not everyone who says to me, 'Lord, Lord,' will enter the kingdom of heaven, but only the one who does the will of my Father who is in heaven. Many will say to me on that day, 'Lord, Lord, did we not prophesy in your name and in your name drive out demons and in your name perform many miracles?' Then I will tell them plainly, 'I never knew you. Away from me, you evildoers!'" (Matthew 7:21-23)

I want to be recognized by Jesus when that day comes and I call out to Him. I also want my friends, family, and everyone else to realize the glory of that moment at their appointed times. However, I believe Billy Graham and W.A. Criswell were actually optimists based on what I found next.

I'm a bit of a data nerd and love looking for the stories in the numbers, so I set out to see if the data aligned with my fears. When I considered ways to measure someone's faith, I thought about what Jesus said was the most important thing. Mark 12:30-31 records it like this: "'Love the Lord your God with all your heart and with all your soul and with all your mind and with all your strength.' … 'Love your neighbor as yourself.' There is no commandment greater than these." Love _____ and love _____, to make it simple.

How do we do this? Well, it sounds simple enough, but it's actually counterintuitive to everything the world would tell us, which sounds more like "you do you, man." The primary difference between the two philosophies is selfish versus unselfish. This makes sense because our God is a giving God. After all, He so loved the world that He gave us His one and only Son (John 3:16). This means that we are never more like God than when we give of ourselves. If I want to figure out just how deep our faith runs, one metric I could look at would be how giving we are, not just of our finances, but also of our time and our talents since these are resources we can offer as well.

I also looked at a number of other studies with the hope of illuminating our real level of faith. Does it go beyond the surface level? Here's what I found through my research.

Let's start by looking at those who identify as Christians and seeing if that number is growing at a healthy rate.

In U.S., roughly three-in-ten adults now religiously unaffiliated

% of U.S. adults who identify with ...

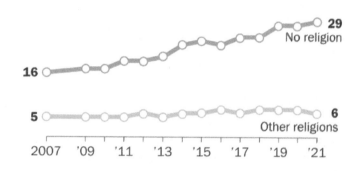

78%

63%
Christianity

29
No religion

16

5

6
Other religions

2007 '09 '11 '13 '15 '17 '19 '21

Note: Those who did not answer are not shown.
Source: Data from 2020-21 based on Pew Research Center's
National Public Opinion Reference Surveys (NPORS), conducted
online and by mail among a nationally representative group of
respondents recruited using address-based sampling. All data from
2019 and earlier from the Center's random-digit-dial telephone
surveys, including the 2007 and 2014 Religious Landscape Studies.
See Methodology for details.
"About Three-in-Ten U.S. Adults Are Now Religiously Unaffiliated"

PEW RESEARCH CENTER

According to Gallup, "over 90% of the adult population identified as Christian" in the 1950s. Considering these numbers and our present society, what do you believe this means for the future?

_____

_____

_____

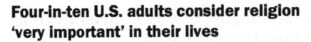

Four-in-ten U.S. adults consider religion 'very important' in their lives

% of U.S. adults who say religion is _____ important in their life

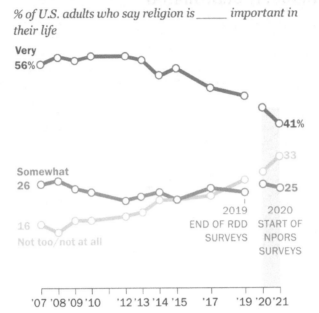

Note: Those who did not answer are not shown. Self-administered surveys (like the NPORS) may produce slightly lower estimates of religion's importance than interviewer-administered surveys (like random-digit-dial, or RDD, telephone surveys). For additional details, see "Measuring Religion in Pew Research Center's American Trends Panel."
Source: Data from 2020-21 based on Pew Research Center's National Public Opinion Reference Surveys (NPORS), conducted online and by mail among a nationally representative group of respondents recruited using address-based sampling. All other estimates come from RDD telephone surveys, including the 2007 and 2014 Religious Landscape Studies; see Methodology for details.
"About Three-in-Ten U.S. Adults Are Now Religiously Unaffiliated"

PEW RESEARCH CENTER

How important is religion in our lives? Only 41% of people even consider religion very important in their lives. That means that many people claim to be Christian but admit that it doesn't really mean much to them. What role does your faith play in your everyday decisions? What do you think is the cause for the disconnect between what we say we believe and what we do?

_____

_____

_____

White evangelicals, Jews and atheists more likely than other groups to see conflict between their own religious beliefs and mainstream American culture

How much conflict, if any, is there between your own religious beliefs and mainstream American culture?

	NET A great deal/ some	A great deal	Some	NET Not much/ no conflict	Not much	No conflict at all	No answer
	%	%	%	%	%	%	%
All U.S. adults	**42**	13	29	**57**	32	25	**2=100**
Christian	**45**	15	31	**53**	32	21	**2**
Protestant	**49**	18	31	**50**	30	19	**2**
White evangelical	**66**	29	37	**32**	23	10	**1**
White, not evang.	**36**	7	29	**62**	39	23	**2**
Black Protestant	**35**	10	25	**62**	34	28	**3**
Catholic	**37**	8	29	**62**	35	26	**1**
White	**40**	9	31	**59**	36	23	**1**
Hispanic	**32**	5	27	**67**	33	33	**2**
Jewish	**52**	17	35	**46**	33	13	**2**
Unaffiliated	**34**	9	25	**65**	32	33	**1**
Atheist	**57**	19	38	**42**	25	18	**<1**
Agnostic	**31**	6	25	**68**	33	35	**<1**
Nothing in particular	**27**	6	21	**71**	34	37	**2**
Republican/lean Rep.	**48**	18	30	**50**	28	22	**2**
Democrat/lean Dem.	**37**	8	29	**62**	34	27	**1**
White	**46**	14	31	**53**	32	22	**1**
Black	**33**	11	22	**64**	33	31	**3**
Hispanic	**33**	7	26	**65**	28	36	**2**

Note: Figures may not add to 100% or to subtotals indicated due to rounding. Blacks and whites are not Hispanic; Hispanics are of any race.
Source: Survey conducted Feb. 4-15, 2020, among U.S. adults.
"White Evangelicals See Trump as Fighting for Their Beliefs, Though Many Have Mixed Feelings About His Personal Conduct"

PEW RESEARCH CENTER

What effect does American mainstream culture have on Christianity? 53% of Christians don't seem concerned about the stark contrast between our American lifestyle and the biblical worldview. In what ways does our American lifestyle differ from a biblical worldview?

_____

_____

_____

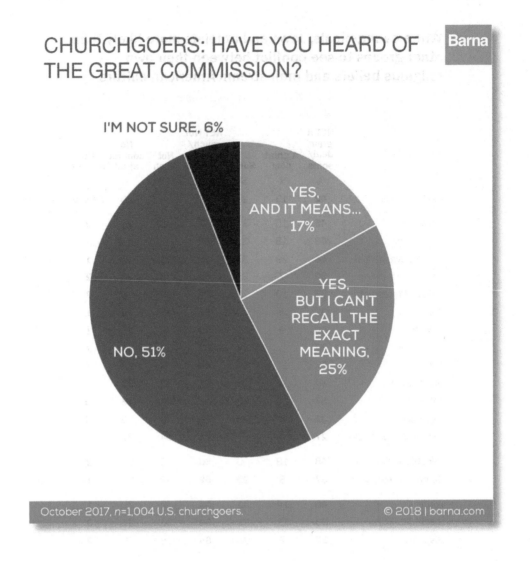

CHURCHGOERS: HAVE YOU HEARD OF THE GREAT COMMISSION?

Barna

I'M NOT SURE, 6%

YES, AND IT MEANS... 17%

YES, BUT I CAN'T RECALL THE EXACT MEANING, 25%

NO, 51%

October 2017, n=1,004 U.S. churchgoers.

© 2018 | barna.com

How many Christians have heard of the Great Commission? This is our purpose as given by Jesus, so we should know it, right? 82% of Christians did not know what the Great Commission was.

Evangelical Protestants get the most questions right about Christianity; Jews are most well-versed in world religions

Average number of questions answered correctly

	Total (out of 32)	Bible and Christianity (out of 14)	Other world religions (out of 13)
Total	14.2	7.7	4.3
Christian	14.2	8.2	3.9
Protestant	14.3	8.4	3.8
Evangelical	15.5	9.3	4.0
Mainline	14.6	8.1	4.2
Historically black	9.7	6.0	2.4
Catholic	14.0	7.9	4.0
Mormon	13.9	8.5	3.3
Jewish	18.7	8.0	7.7
Unaffiliated	13.7	6.8	4.5
Atheist	17.9	8.6	6.1
Agnostic	17.0	8.2	5.8
Nothing in particular	11.4	5.8	3.7

Note: Five questions about nonbelief, the religious demography of the U.S. and religion in the U.S. Constitution are included in the total column but are not included in either the Bible and Christianity questions or the world religion questions.
Source: Survey conducted Feb. 4-19, 2019, among U.S. adults.
"What Americans Know About Religion"

PEW RESEARCH CENTER

The data up to this point begs the question: how well do Christians actually understand the Bible? If the graphic above was a test, we would fail miserably. On average, Christians only correctly answered 8.2 out of 14 questions about the Bible and Christianity. If you had to rate yourself honestly, how well would you say you know the Bible?

_____

_____

_____

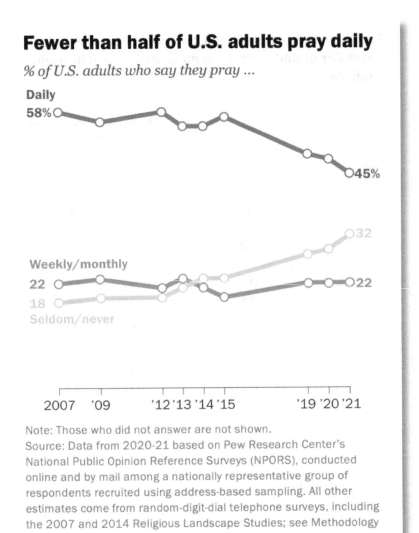

Fewer than half of U.S. adults pray daily

% of U.S. adults who say they pray ...

Daily
58%
45%

Weekly/monthly
22
22

32

18
Seldom/never

2007 '09   '12 '13 '14 '15   '19 '20 '21

Note: Those who did not answer are not shown.
Source: Data from 2020-21 based on Pew Research Center's
National Public Opinion Reference Surveys (NPORS), conducted
online and by mail among a nationally representative group of
respondents recruited using address-based sampling. All other
estimates come from random-digit-dial telephone surveys, including
the 2007 and 2014 Religious Landscape Studies; see Methodology
for details.
"About Three-in-Ten U.S. Adults Are Now Religiously Unaffiliated"

PEW RESEARCH CENTER

How often do we reach out to our Creator, God, in prayer? If we really believe that He exists and hears our prayers, shouldn't the daily number be higher than 45%? And this number is plummeting.

A quarter of U.S. adults say they attend religious services at least weekly

Aside from weddings and funerals, how often do you attend religious services?

	2020 %	2021 %
Monthly or more	**33**	**31**
At least once a week	26	25
Once or twice a month	7	7
Few times a year or less	**66**	**68**
Few times a year	19	15
Seldom	23	26
Never	24	27
Refused	**1**	**1**
	100	**100**

Source: Pew Research Center's National Public Opinion Reference Surveys (NPORS), conducted online and by mail among a nationally representative group of U.S. adults recruited using address-based sampling.
"About Three-in-Ten U.S. Adults Are Now Religiously Unaffiliated"

PEW RESEARCH CENTER

How often are we attending church to learn and grow in our faith? Nearly seven out of ten U.S. adults say they only attend religious services a few times per year or less. 27% of people never go.

Reflect on your own worshiping practices. Are you content with your level of participation in church or individual worship, and if so, do you feel like you are experiencing the fullness of God in your life?

_____

_____

_____

_____

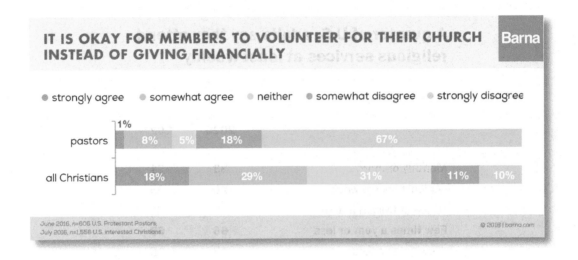

IT IS OKAY FOR MEMBERS TO VOLUNTEER FOR THEIR CHURCH INSTEAD OF GIVING FINANCIALLY | Barna

● strongly agree ● somewhat agree ● neither ● somewhat disagree ● strongly disagree

pastors	1% / 8% / 5% / 18%	67%
all Christians	18% / 29%	31% / 11% / 10%

June 2016, n=606 U.S. Protestant Pastors,
July 2016, n=1,556 U.S. Interested Christians.

© 2018 | barna.com

Is it any wonder our idea of giving is skewed? Volunteering is good, but doesn't our faith call us to both giving and serving?

THE ULTIMATE FINANCIAL GOAL FOR LIFE, BY GENERATION | Barna

	% all Christians	% Millennials	% Gen X	% Boomers	% Elders
1. Provide for my family	22	31	18	18	13
2. Support the lifestyle I want	15	14	17	13	7
3. Meet my obligations and needs	13	8	15	15	16
4. Be content	13	11	14	13	14
5. Give charitably	11	8	11	15	18
6. Serve God with my money	10	10	9	11	19
7. Establish a financial legacy	7	7	8	6	6
8. Be debt-free	6	6	5	6	4
9. Show my talent / hard work	2	4	1	1	-
10. Other	2	1	2	2	4

n=1,556 (U.S. Interested Christians) | July 2016

It would appear that our priorities are out of order with a biblical worldview. Only 21% of Christians prioritize serving God with their money or giving charitably. Barna Research also found in 2007 that among all born-again Christian adults, only 9% contributed one-tenth or more of their income.

SELF-REPORTED DONATIONS FOR LAST YEAR, BY GENERATION

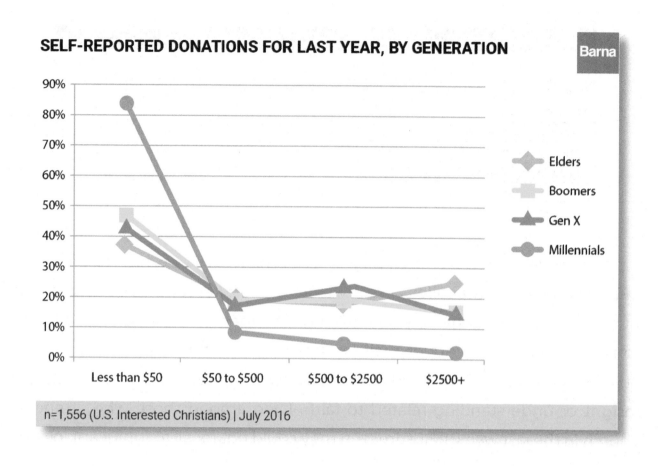

n=1,556 (U.S. Interested Christians) | July 2016

On average, older Christians donated more money to their churches than younger Christians. Whether you do or do not donate money, what is your perception of generosity?

_____

_____

_____

_____

_____

_____

_____

_____

_____

_____

Church Experiences, by Generation				
Generation >	Mosaics (18-27)	Busters (28-46)	Boomers (47-65)	Elders (66-plus)
Feel part of a group that cares for each other	47%	71%	71%	70%
Felt a real and personal connection with God	56%	62%	70%	71%
Gained new spiritual insight or understanding	35%	37%	40%	43%
Church puts a lot of emphasis on serving poor	30%	41%	41%	43%
Attending church affected my life greatly	20%	23%	28%	33%

Source: Barna Group | OmniPoll℠ | www.barna.org

What role does the church play in all of this? Only one-fifth to one-third of people feel that their life is greatly affected by attending church, and that number is significantly smaller among younger churchgoers. According to Barna, when asked about their last church visit, "three out of five church attenders (61%) said they could not remember a significant or important new insight or understanding related to faith. Even among those who attended church in the last week, half admitted they could not recall a significant insight they had gained."

Additionally, Barna reported, "When pastors described their notion of significant, faith-driven life change, the vast majority (more than four out [of] five) focused on salvation but ignored issues related to lifestyle or spiritual maturity... [According to the pastors surveyed,] whether or not people have accepted Jesus Christ as their savior is the sole or primary indicator of "life transformation," regardless of whether their life after such a decision produces spiritual fruit." Where does the church's responsibility end and your responsibility begin with regards to growing in your faith?

_____

_____

_____

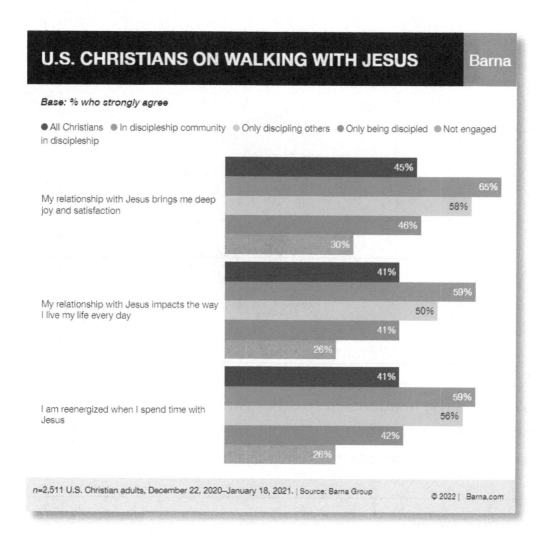

n=2,511 U.S. Christian adults, December 22, 2020–January 18, 2021. | Source: Barna Group

© 2022 | Barna.com

What about a personal relationship with Jesus and the impact of that? Less than half of Christians are experiencing deep joy and satisfaction from their relationship with Jesus. How can this be? What do you feel in your relationship to Jesus Christ? How do you define deep joy and satisfaction?

_____

_____

_____

_____

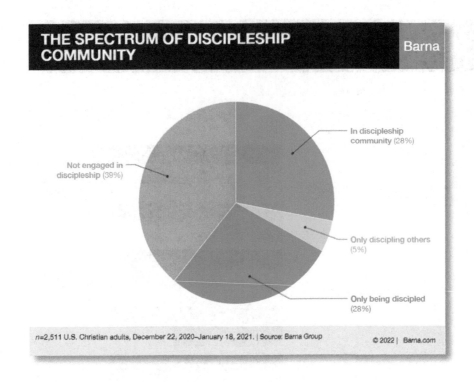

THE SPECTRUM OF DISCIPLESHIP COMMUNITY — Barna

In discipleship community (28%)

Not engaged in discipleship (39%)

Only discipling others (5%)

Only being discipled (28%)

n=2,511 U.S. Christian adults, December 22, 2020–January 18, 2021. | Source: Barna Group   © 2022 | Barna.com

What about the relationship to others and discipleship? More than a third of Christians are not engaged in discipleship. Where do you fall on this chart? What have been your experiences with discipleship?

_____

_____

_____

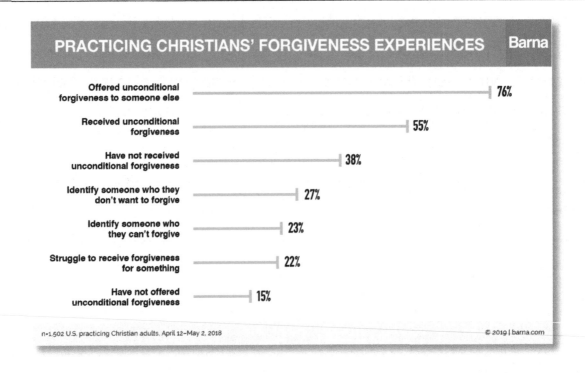

PRACTICING CHRISTIANS' FORGIVENESS EXPERIENCES — Barna

Offered unconditional forgiveness to someone else — 76%

Received unconditional forgiveness — 55%

Have not received unconditional forgiveness — 38%

Identify someone who they don't want to forgive — 27%

Identify someone who they can't forgive — 23%

Struggle to receive forgiveness for something — 22%

Have not offered unconditional forgiveness — 15%

n=1,502 U.S. practicing Christian adults. April 12–May 2, 2018   © 2019 | barna.com

How are we doing at living out the core beliefs of our Christian faith? According to the graph above, at least one fourth of all Christians can identify someone they either don't want to or can't forgive.

"Forgiveness is central to Christianity," says Brooke Hempell, Barna's senior vice president of research. "It's what distinguishes it from any other religious faith. We are reconciled to God through Jesus' sacrifice, and in response, we should be agents of reconciliation in every aspect of our lives. If Christians struggle to extend or receive forgiveness, not only do their relationships suffer, [but] the Church's witness is marred."

What can we surmise from the above data? There is a major disconnect with what we say we believe and how we live it out. Either we don't know so we can't really believe, or we don't care enough to be faithful. Maybe it's a bit of both, but I would like to believe that we've just been lulled into complacency by the world around us and that we can change all of this by slowing down for a moment to really know and experience God. If not, the gap between mind and heart will continue to grow, and our children will become increasingly disenfranchised from the church because it appears that nobody seems to actually believe what they say they believe.

The good news is that there is another way to live a new life that is so much more fruitful. The Bible speaks of a _____ "which transcends all understanding [and] will guard your hearts and your minds" in Paul's letter to the Philippians. He writes about this idea of living without anxiety and goes on to give us the recipe thereafter. It starts with how we think, but it requires us to reach beyond the surface level.

Philippians 4:4-8 establishes the foundation of our Transcend program and our prayer for each of you: "Rejoice in the Lord always. I will say it again: Rejoice! Let your gentleness be evident to all. The Lord is near. Do not be anxious about anything, but in every situation, by prayer and petition, with thanksgiving, present your requests to God. And the peace of God, which transcends all understanding, will guard your hearts and your minds in Christ Jesus. Finally, brothers and sisters, whatever is true, whatever is noble, whatever is right, whatever is pure, whatever is lovely, whatever is admirable—if anything is excellent or praiseworthy—think about such things."

WHAT WE ARE TREATING

Mind	&	Heart	→	Character/ outcome
• Unbelief and Fears • Treated with the assurance of the Word of God, leading to faith in Christ.		• Bitterness and Resentment • Treated with forgiveness, leading to love because of hope in Christ.		• Surrender, leading to Christ-like character which honors God. OR • Dissobedience, stemming from self-serving and self-promoting nature which leads to sin.

REFLECTION QUESTIONS

1. Which statistic from this chapter most surprised you?

2. Are you confident that your faith reaches beyond the surface level?

3. Have you struggled with forgiveness?

CHAPTER 2

BEYOND THE SURFACE OF GOD'S STORY

If we are to have faith that goes beyond the surface level, we need to stop expecting the church to do the work for us and begin with the knowledge to have an unshakable foundation. Let us be knowers and not just believers. Let us fill in the gaps where we made assumptions along the way. We make these assumptions when we allow the truth to be a mixture of our Christian faith and what society and culture want us to buy into. The church can even unknowingly facilitate these assumptions.

I grew up attending Catholic church and made many assumptions about other religions and even other denominations of Christianity. I didn't understand, and nobody seemed to be asking or answering the questions. So, I moved on with my own assumptions in order to make sense of the world around me. My school classes taught me about evolution and history, and then I made assumptions around those. I didn't understand the Bible well enough and made assumptions there, too. All the while, I created gaps that did not allow my faith to run beyond the surface level, and the truth became a sort of moving target somewhere in the middle of all of it. I have found that many other Christians have had similar experiences as well. A good example of this is the common belief that if you do more good than bad, then surely God will let you into heaven. This sounds nice on the surface but is simply not true according to the Bible.

This means we need to start by defining truth and understanding just how easily it can be distorted. How well do we actually know God's story? Provided in the appendix are resources that can help you close the gaps. Take some time to review them to strengthen your faith foundation.

All of this is meant to build you up with what you need in order to be a knower. You need to know there is a God. You need to know that the Bible is true, all of it, and it's God's own expression of His love to us. You need to know that Jesus is who he said he is. And you need to know how your story fits into His story. Without knowing these things, we cannot have a deep sense of _____ and lasting _____.

How do we know what we know? Let's start with how easily we can be tricked and just how these gaps in knowledge are created. We first need to recognize that everyone has the ability to develop their own worldview as a result of their experiences, and these experiences can vary greatly from one person to the next.

It's actually pretty easy to be tricked or miss part of a story. Consider that the average person has over _____ thoughts in a day. We can easily and quickly get off track.

The point is that _____ matters, but it does not define the truth! There is massive power in our thoughts and how we perceive the things around us. Our limited view can control the narrative we believe even as it relates to God. Our perspective is what shapes our worldview and ultimately our _____.

Can truth be different from one person to the next?

We need to take some time through this process to reconcile our personal story and determine if it has been shaped by truth or only what we have perceived as truth. How our stories continue depends on what we determine to be truth.

The world has never been more divided on what truth is than it is today. Again, for some people, truth is simply a collection of beliefs which we have learned along the way. What happens if we are completely misled or if we only know pieces of the truth? It is our responsibility to seek and confirm what truth really is.

It's time to reverse the way we think. Truth should frame our worldview and beliefs, which should then help us control how we feel. Instead, we allow our feelings and thoughts to control what we believe, and this incorrectly shapes our worldview.

Don't believe me? Think about this for a moment: secular thinking suggests that humans are creatures that result from random chance, and some believe that the key to life is fulfillment by self-actualization because humans are inherently good by nature. However, the _____ directly contradicts this by telling us that we are purposely created in the image of a loving God for a relationship to Him and each other, but because of our brokenness resulting from free will, we are sinful and in need of a savior.

We each must conclude and commit to what is actually the truth. Have you heard of apologetics before? Apologetics, in Christianity, is the intellectual defense of the truth of the Christian religion, usually considered a branch of theology. It asks and answers the question, "Is the Bible and the story contained within true? All of it?" The appendix of this workbook includes a ton of apologetics information for your reference. You should use the time between sessions to review this material and become familiar with it. We want you to be comfortable in defending your faith, not so you can argue with others, but so you can be a knower who experiences joy and peace.

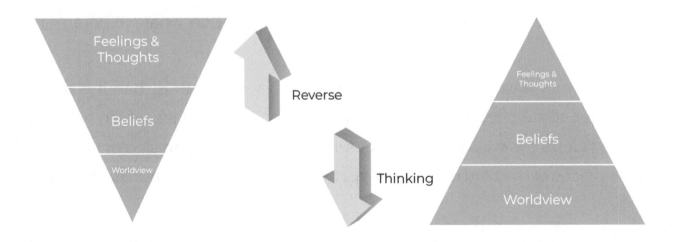

1. What assumptions have you made about faith?

2. Where did these assumptions come from?

3. Do these assumptions skew your perception of the truth?

I consistently point to three subjects when I find myself in discussions which require me to defend my Biblical worldview: _____, _____-_____, and the mathematical probability of Jesus fulfilling even just eight out of the 456 prophecies of the Messiah. These three subjects are remarkable proof of God and that Jesus is who He said He was. It's important to understand that we don't need to know every detail of God's story—just enough to conclude that He is very real.

The next step is to answer the question: "Is the Bible an accurate historical documentation or simply a collection of unverified stories?" You will find what you need to answer this question in the appendix as well. With all of this, we only need to decide how we will respond to the information.

Jesus said, "I am the way and the truth and the life. No one comes to the Father except through me" (John 14:6). Do you know this? Does it cause you to chase Him down and not just follow Him?

If we accept a biblical worldview, everything should change. Our lives should look and feel radically different from those who do not believe. We should view the world differently and respond to situations differently. We should act differently in relationships, marriages, and parenting. The biblical worldview offers hope and peace beyond circumstance, so we should be the most joyful people on the planet, right?

This is why we slow everything down to the basics for a few moments.

The truth is this:

1. God exists.

2. The Bible, the vehicle of His self-revelation, is utterly reliable.

3. Faith in Jesus Christ is the only way to hope and peace while on this earth and to eternity in Heaven.

REFLECTION QUESTIONS

1. Are you a believer or a knower?

God's Story Simplified

1. **God _____ you.**

   a. "So, God created man in his own image, in the image of God he created him; male and female he created them" (Genesis 1:27).

   b. "For you created my inmost being; you knit me together in my mother's womb" (Psalm 139:13).

2. **God _____ you and wants a personal relationship with you.**

   a. "For God so loved the world that he gave his one and only Son, that whoever believes in him shall not perish but have eternal life" (John 3:16).

   b. "How great is the love the Father has lavished on us, that we should be called children of God! And that is what we are! The reason the world does not know us is that it did not know him" (1 John 3:1).

3. **God has a divine** _____ **for your life.**

    a. "For I know the plans I have for you," declares the LORD, "plans to prosper you and not to harm you, plans to give you hope and a future" (Jeremiah 29:11).

    b. "I have come that they may have life, and have it to the full" (John 10:10).

Our Problem

1. **We have a natural desire to** _____ **and ignore God's principles for living.**

    a. "The acts of the sinful nature are obvious: sexual immorality, impurity, and debauchery; idolatry and witchcraft; hatred, discord, jealousy, fits of rage, selfish ambition, dissensions, factions and envy; drunkenness, orgies, and the like. I warn you, as I did before, that those who live like this will not inherit the kingdom of God" (Galatians 5:19-21).

2. **The Bible calls this attitude** _____.

    a. "We all, like sheep, have gone astray, each of us has turned to his own way; and the LORD has laid on him the iniquity of us all" (Isaiah 53:6).

    b. "If we claim to be without sin, we deceive ourselves and the truth is not in us" (1 John 1:8).

3. **Sin** _____ **us from God.**

    a. "But your iniquities have separated you from your God; your sins have hidden his face from you, so that he will not hear" (Isaiah 59:2).

    b. "For all have sinned and fall short of the glory of God" (Romans 3:23).

4. **Sin** _____ **and hurts us.**

   a. "For what I do is not the good I want to do; no, the evil I do not want to do—this I keep on doing" (Romans 7:19).

   b. "I see another law at work in the members of my body, waging war against the law of my mind and making me a prisoner of the law of sin at work within my members. What a wretched man I am! Who will rescue me from this body of death? Thanks be to God-through Jesus Christ our Lord!" (Romans 7:23-25)

   c. When our relationship with God is not right, it eventually causes problems in every area of our lives—marriage, career, relationships, finances, personal satisfaction, etc.

God's Solution

God loved us so much that even while we were sinners, He still wanted to extend to us a relationship with Him and offered the ultimate solution.

1. **Jesus is the only** _____ **to our sin problem!**

   a. Jesus Christ said of himself, "I AM THE WAY, the Truth, and the Life. No one comes to the Father, except THROUGH ME!" (John 14:6)

   b. "For there is one God and one mediator between God and men, the man Jesus Christ" (1 Timothy 2:5).

   c. God Himself came to earth as a human being to bring us back to Himself. If any other way had worked, Jesus Christ would not have had to come.

2. **Jesus** _____ **on the cross and rose from the grave!**

   a. "But God demonstrates His own love for us in this: While we were still sinners, Christ died for us" (Romans 5:8).

b. "... that Christ died for our sins according to the Scriptures, that he was buried, that he was raised on the third day according to the Scriptures, and that he appeared to Peter, and then to the Twelve" (1 Corinthians 15:3-5).

3. **Jesus paid the penalty for our sin and _____ the gap between God and people.**

   a. "For the wages of sin is death, but the gift of God is eternal life in Christ Jesus our Lord" (Romans 6:23).

   b. "For Christ died for sins once for all, the righteous for the unrighteous, to bring you to God" (1 Peter 3:18).

4. **The only way to receive salvation is by _____ through faith.**

   a. "For it is by grace you have been saved, through faith—and this is not from yourselves, it is the gift of God—not by works, so that no one can boast" (Ephesians 2:8-9).

   b. GRACE is God's part. FAITH is man's part. (But what is true faith?)

   c. "Now faith is being sure of what we hope for and certain of what we do not see" (Hebrews 11:1).

   d. "And without faith it is impossible to please God, because anyone who comes to him must believe that he exists and that he rewards those who earnestly seek him" (Hebrews 11:6).

   e. "You see that his faith and his actions were working together, and his faith was made complete by what he did" (James 2:22).

Our Response

The New Testament both commands and shows how we should respond to God's offer of forgiveness. This faith response includes these aspects:

_____ in Jesus. It is recognizing that he is God's Son; he came as a man, died for us, and rose from the dead (1 Corinthians 15:3-5). It is having faith, which is placing our total trust in him (John 3:16). It is NOT simply intellectual assent; Biblical faith includes obedience to Him (James 2:14-24).

_____ that Jesus is Lord. It is publicly declaring that you are now living your life for Jesus (Romans 10:9-10). It is NOT simply saying that you believe in Jesus, but that He is in charge of your life (2 Corinthians 9:13). It is never denying him, even when people and situations pressure you (Mathew 10:32-33).

_____ of sin. It is asking for forgiveness while we walk toward Jesus and away from sin (Acts 2:38). It is NOT achieving perfection before you follow Jesus, but it is changing your heart and mind, turning from your old way of life (Acts 26:20). It is NOT merely being sorry for what you have done but getting right with God (2 Corinthians 7:10-11).

Being _____ into Christ. It is for believers only and it is properly done by immersion in water (Acts 8:36-38). It is NOT magic water, but it is commanded as part of the faith response to the gift of God's grace (Acts 2:38, Galatians 3:26-27). It is our pledge to God that pictures Jesus' resurrection in our life (1 Peter 3:21, Romans 6:4).

Remaining _____. It is following Jesus for the rest of your life (Revelation 2:10). It is growing in our relationship with Him (Philippians 1:6, 2:12). It is staying connected to Jesus and bearing fruit for Him (John 15:5-8). It does NOT mean you will never sin again but that you will not deliberately continue in sin (Hebrews 10:26). It is NOT earning grace, but it is a response to grace (Romans 6:1-2).

Realizing that God loves me and created me to have a personal relationship with Him and that my sin makes me guilty and separates me from God. I have responded in the following ways:

I **BELIEVE** that Jesus Christ is the Son of God and that He died for me upon the cross.

I have **CONFESSED** Jesus to be the Lord (leader) and Savior (forgiver) of my life.

I have **REPENTED** of my sin, turning from my old way of living to God.

I have been **BAPTIZED** (immersed) in obedience to Christ's example and command.

REFLECTION QUESTIONS

1. The outline above is a simple summary of the Christian Faith. Have you accepted each aspect of it and responded accordingly?

2. Do you know the outline well enough to lead someone else through it?

3. Why is apologetics so important?

CHAPTER 3

BEYOND THE SURFACE OF YOUR STORY

You have likely heard of making changes from the inside out. This is why I start by questioning what you really believe as opposed to focusing on behaviors and habits. Changing behaviors and habits can be difficult if you're not really convinced by a good reason. In order to have the greatest impact, it's important that we understand how God designed us so that we can strive for whole health.

Scripture tells us, "May God himself, the God of peace, sanctify you through and through. May your whole spirit, soul and body be kept blameless at the coming of our Lord Jesus Christ" (1 Thessalonians 5:23).

God created us with three parts—spirit, soul, and body—and we need to give attention to all three. In simple terms, we are _____ beings who have a _____ and live in a physical _____.

+ **Our _____ is the breath which God breathed into us.** It provides meaning and purpose. This spirit guides us as we allow it to and helps us determine right from wrong. There is only one thing made to fit here. This is a God-shaped hole which must be filled through a relationship to the Creator. We only need to be willing to allow God to activate His Holy Spirit in us. Surrendering to this is so difficult but also provides freedom, peace, and joy.

+ **Our _____ is our mind, will, and emotions working to develop our character and reflect our personality.** Emotions are complex and difficult to process when we set expectations which are not met. There is work we must do to process our thoughts, reasoning, emotions, beliefs, feelings, attitudes, memories, and so on. The soul can stand in the way of truly connecting with God as we struggle to take control of our lives.

+ **Our _____ is the physical cells, organs, nerves, and so**

on which make up our appearance, physical abilities, and senses. Physical experiences are simple to process. For example, if you burn your hand, it hurts. It is easy for us to understand that if we don't take care of our body, it will give us trouble and break down. We would do good to remember that the same holds true for our spirit and soul.

The body is pretty straightforward to care for, and most of us understand what we should be doing. Eat healthy and exercise, and if you get hurt, go to the doctor.

REFLECTION QUESTIONS

1. In what ways do you physically care for your body?

2. Do you view spiritual health as important as physical health? Why or why not?

3. What often prohibits you from taking care of your spiritual health?

Mental health is a little more complex and was less explored until around one hundred years ago. The mental health industry was built around trying to care for WWII vets dealing with a host of issues like PTSD, and it was mostly funded by the government. This painted the industry in a negative light and made talking about our problems embarrassing. Thankfully, great progress has been made, but we still have a long way to go.

Spiritual health has largely been shaped by our parents and their parents. Sadly, many think we can nurture this part of our being with a one-hour church service a few times per month and then wonder why we are spiritually starving.

1. In what ways do you care for your mental health?

2. What is your perception of mental health, and why?

3. Would you describe yourself as "spiritually starving"?

Each of these three parts can also greatly impact the other, making whole health near impossible to obtain. For example, neglecting your physical health can have a terrible effect on your mental health. Similarly, struggling with mental health issues can impact your physical health. Neglecting your spiritual health can impact both mental and physical health. You can see the pattern here—it's all connected.

To make matters more difficult, the church is not well-equipped to discuss mental health issues, and the mental health field is not allowed to address spiritual issues unless invited to do so. This only serves to feed the gap between what we think, what we believe, and what we do.

Interconnection of Spirit, Soul & Body

1 Thessalonians 5:23   May God himself, the God of peace, sanctify you through and through. May your whole spirit, soul, and body be kept blameless at the coming of our Lord Jesus Christ.

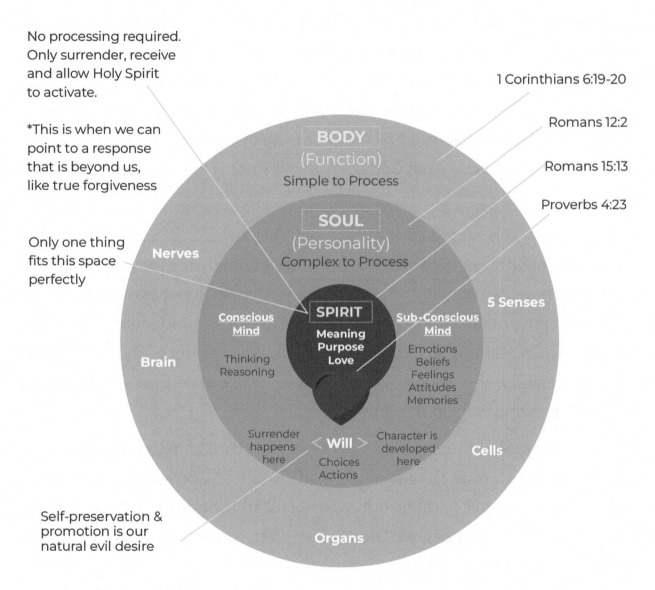

No processing required. Only surrender, receive and allow Holy Spirit to activate.

*This is when we can point to a response that is beyond us, like true forgiveness

Only one thing fits this space perfectly

1 Corinthians 6:19-20

Romans 12:2

Romans 15:13

Proverbs 4:23

BODY (Function) Simple to Process

SOUL (Personality) Complex to Process

Nerves

Brain

SPIRIT Meaning Purpose Love

5 Senses

Conscious Mind Thinking Reasoning

Sub-Conscious Mind Emotions Beliefs Feelings Attitudes Memories

Surrender happens here

< **Will** > Choices Actions

Character is developed here

Cells

Self-preservation & promotion is our natural evil desire

Organs

We are <u>spiritual</u> beings who have a <u>soul</u> & live in a <u>body</u>.

This diagram has been adapted from an original diagram by Fletcher available at https://www.faithandhealthconnection.org/the_connection/spirit-soul-and-body/ and is used with permission.

Try now to imagine the peace of God, which transcends all understanding, guarding your heart and mind as Paul describes in the Bible. You may remember that he alludes to the recipe for necessary change as well. In Philippians 4:8, he states, "Finally, brothers and sisters, whatever is true, whatever is noble, whatever is right, whatever is pure, whatever is lovely, whatever is admirable—if anything is excellent or praiseworthy—think about such things." Could it really be this easy? Consider another verse, also by the Apostle Paul. This time, he is writing his letter to the Romans and says, "Do not conform to the pattern of this world, but be transformed by the renewing of your mind. Then you will be able to test and approve what God's will is—his good, pleasing and perfect will" (Romans 12:2).

First of all, this suggests that it is possible to _____ our minds. This was a huge statement for the time. It's only in recent years that it has been proven we can actually do this. It's what we now know as neuroplasticity, the ability of the brain to form and reorganize synaptic connections, especially in response to learning or experience. If you love science and need more information about this, I suggest looking into Dr. Caroline Leaf's writings. She has done amazing work in this area.

Another verse that comes to mind is Proverbs 23:7 from the New King James Bible: "As a man thinks in his heart, so is he." Conversely, don't forget that garbage in equals garbage out. We must start by intentionally consuming the word and promises of God. Then, we need to run everything else through our biblical worldview filter.

From 2 Corinthians 10:5: "We demolish arguments and every pretension that sets itself up against the knowledge of God, and we take captive every thought to make it obedient to Christ."

I recommend you take time to listen to one of my favorite messages on the concept of this peace which transcends all understanding delivered by Tim Keller.

I recommend following it with a few minutes of worship by listening to this beautiful rendition of *It Is Well With My Soul* by Audrey Assad.

With this understanding of self and a desire to move towards peace, we move into the workshop part of the program and take a few assessments to gain a better understanding of your story. We do this by looking at your current state, the events that have robbed you of peace, the personality you have developed, the spiritual gifts God has placed in you, and how you relate to others.

On a scale of 0 to 10, how would you rate yourself in the following areas? Please circle one.

no problem = 0

low concern = 1-3

medium concern = 4-6

high concern = 7-9

worst = 10

Physical Health

Diet

0	1	2	3	4	5	6	7	8	9	10

Unhealthy Habits/Behaviors

0	1	2	3	4	5	6	7	8	9	10

Physical Pain/Sickness

0	1	2	3	4	5	6	7	8	9	10

Lack of Exercise and Activity

0	1	2	3	4	5	6	7	8	9	10

Overall Physical Condition

0	1	2	3	4	5	6	7	8	9	10

Mental Health

Depression/Hopelessness

0	1	2	3	4	5	6	7	8	9	10

Anxiety

0	1	2	3	4	5	6	7	8	9	10

Fear (irrational)

0	1	2	3	4	5	6	7	8	9	10

Anger (unhealthy)

0	1	2	3	4	5	6	7	8	9	10

Self Esteem

0	1	2	3	4	5	6	7	8	9	10

Uncontrollable Thoughts

0	1	2	3	4	5	6	7	8	9	10

Stress

0	1	2	3	4	5	6	7	8	9	10

Life Balance (work, family, leisure, etc.)

0	1	2	3	4	5	6	7	8	9	10

Satisfaction in Relationships

0	1	2	3	4	5	6	7	8	9	10

Spiritual Health

Believe in God

Yes	Not Sure	No

Have Accepted Jesus as Lord and Savior

Yes	Not Sure	No

Have Been Baptized by Submersion

Yes	Not Sure	No

Have Spiritual Pain, Unforgiveness, and/or Bitterness

0	1	2	3	4	5	6	7	8	9	10

Reality of God in Your Life

0	1	2	3	4	5	6	7	8	9	10

Regularly Attend Church

0	1	2	3	4	5	6	7	8	9	10

Read the Bible Regularly

0	1	2	3	4	5	6	7	8	9	10

Complete Bible Studies/Devotions Regularly

0	1	2	3	4	5	6	7	8	9	10

Pray Regularly

0	1	2	3	4	5	6	7	8	9	10

Comfortable Praying Out Loud for Others

0	1	2	3	4	5	6	7	8	9	10

Daily Routine Includes Time with God

0	1	2	3	4	5	6	7	8	9	10

Actively Serve Others through Church/Ministry

0	1	2	3	4	5	6	7	8	9	10

Comfortable leading a Life Group or Bible Study

0	1	2	3	4	5	6	7	8	9	10

Struggle with Control

0	1	2	3	4	5	6	7	8	9	10

Financial Stewardship

0	1	2	3	4	5	6	7	8	9	10

Please rate yourself on a scale from 0 to 10, with 0 meaning the least concern and 10 meaning the most concern.

What overall score would you give yourself for physical health? _____

What overall score would you give yourself for mental health? _____

What overall score would you give yourself for spiritual health? _____

Record your scores on the My Story page in the appendix.

Unfortunately, everyone experiences hurting events over the course of their lives. Pain is inevitable. At the root of most emotional pain is likely one of these:

✦ _____

✦ _____

✦ _____

Hurting events generally produce stress, and that stress can be tolerable if there are supportive relationships and resources in place. It can even be positive and produce growth in some cases. However, these events can also produce toxic stress, especially if support structures are nonexistent or lacking. Toxic stress can have long-term impacts on mental, physical, and spiritual health. Mental health counseling and regular medical check-ups should be a source of support in these scenarios.

What many people don't understand is that a healthy spiritual life can have a positive impact on toxic stress too and, in turn, affect mental and physical health. We've already discussed how our physical, mental, and spiritual health each function independently but also overlap and affect one another. A great example of the positive effects of a healthy spiritual life can be found in the book *The Forgiveness Project* by Michael S. Barry. Similarly, an emotionally unhealthy life will block us from obtaining spiritual maturity. Another great read on this topic is *Emotionally Healthy Spirituality* by Peter Scazzero.

Hurting events can be self-inflicted, inflicted by others, or purely circumstantial. A natural byproduct of a hurting event is _____, which by itself is not harmful if processed well. Processing anger well means finding positive outcomes, ways to leverage your feelings for good, and seeing the event through a biblical perspective. When anger is not processed well, it becomes _____, which festers within us and causes damage and destruction to our physical, mental, and spiritual health. If we don't acknowledge and positively process the hurting events in our lives, we will have no chance of experiencing peace "which transcends all understanding" (Philippians 4:7).

While hurting events cannot be avoided, we can completely change the impact they have on us by processing them well and making different choices in how we respond. We tend to react in one of a few ways to hurts:

1. _____ or denying that the hurting event happened or that any feelings around it exist, leading to bitterness

2. _____ or packing the feelings away and trying not to address them, which also leads to bitterness

3. _____ the pain, which can be done verbally and/or nonverbally

Of these, it hopefully seems obvious that expressing anger is the best option. That said, expressing anger can easily go wrong as well. Expressing the anger from a hurting event well involves first realizing that the event happened, then recognizing the feelings associated with the hurt, and finally and most importantly, deciding how to act on it. We can either react negatively by seeking vengeance or retaliating, or we can react positively by focusing on the _____, not the person, and making changes to avoid similar hurts in the future. You may have heard the common saying, "Hate the sin, love the sinner." Verbally expressing pain is common, and we need to take some time before responding in order to avoid responding negatively. Nonverbal expressions are perhaps even more dangerous, ranging from slamming an object on the counter (a mild expression) to abusive acts towards others or self (a more aggressive expression). There are some who will respond in passive aggressive ways, which is also a negative response.

Anger is not bad by itself. Anger is a natural byproduct of a hurting event and a common emotion. Even God gets angry.

It is critical that when we feel anger, we must decide how we will proceed. Will we choose self-preservation and promotion, or will we choose to honor God by _____ our minds and _____ our hearts? This is the critical point at which we determine if we really believe what we say we believe. This is when our life can reflect our faith, provide peace, and begin changing those around us.

Ephesians 4:26 states, "In your anger do not sin," meaning God knows we get angry and is more concerned about how we respond to our anger.

When we choose not to process and express this anger positively, we allow bitterness to take root in our hearts. Bitterness is referenced many times in the Bible and has a dangerous effect on our hearts as we hold onto it. If you've met people who can seem to find the negative in anything, then you have seen the result of bitterness. Low self-esteem is another indicator of bitterness. Maybe you have even battled it yourself at times.

What starts as a hurting event creates anger, and when that anger is not positively processed and festers as bitterness, it always leads to sinfulness. This is the disconnect between what we say we believe and when we act otherwise. What starts with a whispered lie from the enemy or an unforgiving heart, turns into pornography, abuse, affairs, lies, and a host of other sins. This is what perpetuates the cycle of unrest with which our souls desire to part ways so badly. This is what blocks the Holy Spirit from activating Himself in us.

The only things that we can control in this world are our responses. We must choose to avoid bitterness, believe God's word, and _____.

The following is a list of some common types of hurting events and is meant to assist you in recalling yours but is also not exhaustive. We have also provided an area below to add some of your own. Please take the time to consider past hurts which may have been self-inflicted, inflicted by others, or circumstantial while noting that many people do not understand just how many hurting events they have experienced throughout their lives. By looking at these events as a collective, my hope is that you realize how much you've overcome. We recognize that everyone's story is unique. In fact, I have experienced many of the items on the list myself and was surprised the first time I took inventory of them. Also, I know that while two people may experience the same type of event, the experience can greatly vary.

	Myself	Parent/Guardian	My Dependents	Other
Have you experienced divorce?	☐	☐	☐	☐
Have you served time in jail or prison?	☐	☐	☐	☐
Have you experienced mental illness or suicide?	☐	☐	☐	☐
Has anyone close to you threatened to hurt you?	☐	☐	☐	☐
Have you threatened to hurt or actually hurt someone in your family or close to you?	☐	☐	☐	☐
Have you ever experienced emotional abuse or emotionally abused another (e.g. been sworn at, insulted, humiliated, or put down in a way that made you afraid)?	☐	☐	☐	☐
Have you ever experienced physical abuse or physically abused another?	☐	☐	☐	☐
Have you ever experienced sexual abuse or sexually abused another?	☐	☐	☐	☐

	Myself	Parent/Guardian	My Dependents	Other
Have you ever experienced going without food, clothes, shelter, or someone to protect you?	☐	☐	☐	☐
Have you often felt unsupported, unloved, or unprotected?	☐	☐	☐	☐
Have you ever been treated poorly because of your race, sexual orientation, place of birth, disability, religion, immigration status, etc.?	☐	☐	☐	☐
Were you ever in the adoption or foster care system or under the care of guardians for an extended period of time?	☐	☐	☐	☐
Have you ever experienced unhealthy eating habits (bulimia, anorexia, compulsive eating, etc.)?	☐	☐	☐	☐
Have you ever experienced unhealthy addiction (alcohol, drugs, pornography, prescription medications, gambling, cigarettes, etc.)?	☐	☐	☐	☐
Have you ever been betrayed by a friend or family member?	☐	☐	☐	☐
Have you experienced a life-threatening illness?	☐	☐	☐	☐
Have you experienced the loss of a family member or someone close to you?	☐	☐	☐	☐
Have you experienced life-changing financial ruin?	☐	☐	☐	☐
Have you harmed yourself (ex: cutting, substance abuse, etc.)?	☐	☐	☐	☐
Have you cheated on your partner or spouse?	☐	☐	☐	☐
Have you had sex before marriage?	☐	☐	☐	☐
Have you or your spouse had an abortion?	☐	☐	☐	☐
Have you caused damage to someone else's property?	☐	☐	☐	☐

Other: _____

Other: _____

Other: _____

Other: _____

Other: _____

Other: _____

Other: _____

Other: _____

Other: _____

Other: _____

Other: _____

Other: _____

Other: _____

Other: _____

Other: _____

Record any key hurting events on the My Story page in the appendix.

A Better Way of Processing Hurting Events to Avoid Bitterness and Sin

Our nature is of self-preservation and promotion. Instead, try renewing your mind and transforming your heart by positively processing the hurting events.

It all starts with a decision. Feelings will follow. "If you love me, obey my commands" (John 14:15).

WRONG DECISION	RIGHT DECISION
Self-Preservation & Promotion	Renewing & Transforming
Self-Oriented Goals	Pursuing God's Goals
Self-Trust	Believing, Relying on God
Pride, Selfishness	Obeying God's Commands
Fear	Trusting God's Promises
Blame Shift	Hope in God
Bitterness, Rage, Self-Pity	Praying and Forgiving
Suppression, Denial	Focusing on Scripture
Fantasy	Fellowship
Superficiality	Thanking
Detachment, Busyness	Yielding/Surrendering
Manipulation, Control	Accepting
Hopelessness/Depression	Praising God

RESULTS	RESULTS
Focusing on Self/Circumstances	Focused on God/Others
Bondage to Self	Set Free from Self
Further Frustrations	Peace and Joy
Lack of Growth	Maturity
Sinful Attitudes	Godly Attitude
Barren Life	Fruits of the Spirit

Another effect of not processing hurting events well can be the _____ _____ that we develop as a result of believing false narratives from the event itself, words people say, or even generational patterns. For example, we may have experienced emotional abuse by being told that we are worthless and will never amount to anything, or we may have experienced generation patterns of addiction which seem to plague our family. If we do not find our identity in Christ, we may begin to believe the lies that stem from these fears. When this happens, we can find ourselves so gripped by the concern of anything that might validate these false narratives and spend all of our mental energy trying to prove to ourselves and others that it's not accurate.

The devil is a liar and could also be seen as a storyteller, fabricator, fibber, or falsifier. He is a real enemy who would love nothing more than for us to believe those lies and will stop at nothing to do so. John 8:44 says, "He was a murderer from the beginning, not holding to the truth, for there is no truth in him. When he lies, he speaks his native language, for he is a liar and the father of lies."

Every lie we believe about ourselves also says what we believe about God. You can't say that you believe in God but not what He says about you. His promises are absolute, and He paid the ultimate price to prove it!

The good news is that we also have a Savior who has already claimed victory over the devil and his lies. We can claim this same victory in Christ Jesus, and it changes our story immediately. "They triumphed over him by the blood of the Lamb and by the word of their testimony" (Revelation 12:11). Jesus' death on the cross has given us victory. If you read that verse again, it says that our testimony, or story, plays a part in this victory.

The battle to prevail begins in our minds and thoughts with the right decisions. When our thought life is disciplined and healthy (focused on the eternal perspective), our heart will follow with the corresponding emotions.

When this happens, we affect our actions and the outcomes in our lives. Our _____ is truly the only thing we can control in this world. Our response is all God asks of us for the grace, love, and freedom promised to us through Jesus Christ. The only thing in our control is surrendering that very control to Him. This is counterintuitive to us because we have been shaped by a world that says it is culturally wrong to give in to anything.

What are some of the fears or lies that you have battled over the course of your life? Check all that apply. Then, go back through and place a star next to the top three to five.

Fears/Lies List

- [ ] I am insignificant.
- [ ] I am physically flawed.
- [ ] I am mentally flawed.
- [ ] I am emotionally flawed.
- [ ] I was created by chance.
- [ ] I am not good enough to stand before God.
- [ ] I am too sinful.
- [ ] I am generally not accepted.
- [ ] I am unforgivable.
- [ ] I am incomplete.
- [ ] I am unlovable.
- [ ] I am unable to have peace.
- [ ] I am unable to control myself.
- [ ] I am broken and unable to receive healing.
- [ ] I am without purpose in this life.

☐ I am not confident in God's word.

☐ I am defined by my mistakes.

☐ I am rightfully anxious.

☐ I am alone.

☐ I am guilty.

☐ I am weak.

☐ I am incapable.

☐ I am overcome by trying to please others.

Other: _____

The Only Answer to Hurts From Others Is Forgiveness

Let's start with defining forgiveness:

✦ Psychologists generally define forgiveness as a conscious, deliberate decision to release feelings of resentment or vengeance toward a person or group who has harmed you regardless of whether they actually deserve your forgiveness. This has everything to do with our relationship to that person.

✦ Forgiveness, according to the Bible, is correctly understood as God's promise not to count our sins against us. Biblical forgiveness requires repentance on our part (turning away from our old life of sin) and faith in Jesus Christ. This requires a great deal of humility and has everything to do with our relationship to God. We forgive because we are forgiven.

✦ Forgiveness is simply releasing the responsibility to God where it belongs.

Let's also state what forgiveness is NOT:

✦ Forgiveness is not justifying, condoning, understanding, excusing, trivializing, forgetting, saying it's okay, reconciling, denying the hurt, liking an abuser, or letting your boundaries down. It's not letting someone off the hook altogether; it's letting them off your hook and simply leaving them on God's hook. It's not even asking God to forgive them.

Why don't we always forgive? We either don't want to (pride) or don't understand how (knowledge). Even once we understand, motivation is the critical factor, as it's much easier to avoid than take on the work of forgiveness. The problem is that this is where bitterness takes root and begins to destroy us. Avoidance is the opposite of what the Bible teaches, which is to take these challenges head on.

The only factor that brings events from the past into today is the memory of them. When we allow these memories and the bitterness associated with them to control our hearts and minds, we are literally living our lives based on these past events and building walls to "protect" ourselves.

God will move through a willing heart, and forgiveness is the very evidence of God in us. When we forgive, we are most like God. He only needs a wholehearted desire.

It is also impossible to forgive without _____. We are all one bad decision away from disaster at any moment and capable of great evil ourselves. In those moments, we would want others to quickly forgive us, but we so easily forget this. In addition, we would do well to consider how truthful we are about past hurts since we also have the ability to distort our memories and frame scenarios where we are seen in a more positive light in order to avoid additional pain. Until we see ourselves through the lens of humility and others through the lens of God, we will not have the capacity to forgive. Romans 3:23 states, "... for all have sinned and fall short of the glory of God." As Christians, shouldn't we be the best at forgiveness?

It is also impossible to forgive without _____. Hurting people hurt people. Unforgiveness is difficult to hang onto when you pray for those who hurt you. It is understood that forgiveness is also countercultural and counterintuitive to our sinful nature. It is not the normal response. However, unforgiveness is emotional suffocation. We only hurt ourselves by retaining the bitterness and hatred stemming from it.

Focus on what you can learn and how you can grow from the hurt, not "why." Focusing on "why" will only cause frustration and confusion. We don't have the helicopter view that God does and cannot always know the "why." We must trust in Him and choose to respond in a way that honors Him.

1 John 4:20 states, "Whoever claims to love God yet hates a brother or sister is a liar. For whoever does not love their brother and sister, whom they have seen, cannot love God, whom they have not seen."

One other topic that is worth touching on is the idea of self-forgiveness. I personally disagree with the idea of self-forgiveness because it suggests that we have the power to release the debt of our mistakes. That is a job for God and only Him. Instead, why don't we aim for _____? We can and should accept responsibility, confess, repent, and let it become part of our testimony. We should also accept that we are no longer defined by these mistakes because of our Savior Jesus Christ. To believe anything else is to devalue His sacrifice. In fact, we are not truly over our hurts—whether inflicted by others or ourselves—until we can freely speak about them and find victory through Christ in them.

Kintsugi is the Japanese art of golden joinery. "Kin" means gold, and "tsugi" means to patch up. In Japan, broken bowls are put back together with golden paint highlighting their cracks rather than hiding them.

One theory of how kintsugi began is with Japanese shogun Ashikaga Yoshimasa. The story goes that Yoshimasa broke his favorite tea bowl from China, so he sent it back there to have it repaired. However, he did not like how it looked when it came back with staples. He commissioned local potters to see if they could do better.

One potter painstakingly put the pieces back together, but instead of trying to hide the cracks and blemishes, he highlighted them with resin infused with gold powder.

The lesson to be learned here is that the perfect story only exists in one book, and the rest of us need to stop telling ourselves that our story has to be perfect. Embrace the imperfections. Believe it or not, this is what people want to hear and see in you. People want to hear about the time you got something wrong. Be real! Acknowledge the cracks and turn them into beauty that can be admired by others. Christ can be highlighted and shine through our brokenness!

Psalm 147:3: "He heals the brokenhearted and binds up their wounds."

A broken bowl cannot hold anything, but if you allow God to heal your brokenness, you can not only hold what he pours into you, but also overflows into others as well. Remember also that we are only the bowl. He is its contents.

Feelings List

Check all the feelings resulting from hurts you have felt at any time. Then, place a star next to the top three to five that seem consistent for you.

X	Feelings resulting from hurts	During and/or after the event, I believe...
	Abandoned	Those who are close to me have left me.
	Afraid	I was not safe.
	Alone	I have been by myself or on my own, I will be without help or assistance, and/or I have been lonely and isolated.
	Angry	My sense of self was disrespected, and/or I was treated in a way I did not deserve.
	Anxious	I was worried something disastrous would happen.
	Betrayed	Others have been disloyal or unfaithful, others have given up on our relationships, and/or others will share or reveal private information.
	Confused	I will never understand.
	Controlled	I will be dominated, I will be made to submit, what others say goes, and/or I will be treated like a child.
	Deceived	My relationship with others will lack truth, honesty, or trustworthiness; truth will be perverted in order to cheat or defraud me; and/or I will be misled or given false appearances.
	Defective	Something is wrong with me, I'm the problem, and/or I am broken and unlovable.

	Depressed	Life has disappointed me, and/or life will always disappoint me.
	Disappointment	I will let others down, I will disappoint others, and/or others will be disillusioned by me.
	Discouraged	My efforts were not enough.
	Disrespected	I will be treated rudely, my thoughts and opinions will be disregarded, others do not respect me, and/or people have a low opinion of me.
	Embarrassed	I am not liked by others, and/or if others don't like me, my life is over.
	Failure	I am not successful, I will fall short, and/or I won't make the grade.
	Forsaken	God has abandoned me.
	Frustrated	I cannot change my circumstances.
	Giving Up	Nothing I do matters, and/or I am not strong enough to persevere.
	Guilty	It was my fault, and/or my sins define me.
	Helpless/Powerless	I am unable to do anything to change my situation; I am at the end of my power, resources, capacity, or ability to achieve what I want; and/or my life is unmanageable and beyond my control.
	Humiliated	I will be shamed, degraded, and embarrassed; my dignity and self-respect are attacked; and/or I will be made the fool.
	Hurt	I feel great pain within my heart and mind.
	Ignored	Others do not pay attention to me, and/or I feel neglected and invisible.
	Inadequate	Others are more competent than me, and/or I am incapable and ineffective.
	Inferior	Everyone else is better than I am, and/or I am less valuable or important than others.

	Insignificant	I don't matter, I will be of consequence to others, and/or I am not worth mentioning as I am trivial in the eyes of others.
	Intimacy/ Vulnerability	I am afraid of emotionally opening up to others; I will be hurt if I allow my walls to come down; and/or it is uncomfortable to reveal the deepest, most essential parts of who I am.
	Invalidated	Who I am, what I think, what I do, or how I feel doesn't matter.
	Judged	I am always being unfairly criticized or misjudged, others form faulty or negative opinions about me, and/or I am always being evaluated.
	Lonely	I am alone and feel isolated, and/or I do not have a community.
	Misportrayed	I will be portrayed inaccurately, I am described in a negative or untrue manner, and/or people paint a wrong picture of me.
	Misunderstood	Others will fail to understand me correctly, they will get the wrong idea or impression about me, and/or I will be misperceived or misread.
	Not Good Enough	Nothing I do is ever acceptable, satisfactory, or sufficient; the flagpoles keep moving; and/or I won't measure up to people's expectations.
	Phony	I strongly desire to act according to who I say I am, yet I don't know how to reconcile the contradictions that lie within me; and/or others will discover those contradictions within me and believe the worst.
	Rejected	Others do not accept me, and/or I will be pushed away and discarded.
	Sad	I am unhappy.
	Taken advantage of	I will be cheated on, I feel like a "doormat," and/or my goodwill is always exploited.
	Tempted	I give in to my desires without thinking, and/or I have little willpower.

	Threatened	I was unsafe, and/or others do not have my best interests in mind.
	Troubled	My thoughts are tumultuous, and/or I have a general state of unease.
	Unaware	I do not know what is happening in my relationships with people; I'm clueless; and/or personal information seems secretive, hidden, or undisclosed.
	Unfair	I will not be treated equally, I will be asked to do things others are unwilling to do, I will be asked to do things that are unreasonable or excessive, and/or I will be treated differently from others.
	Unforgiveness	I hold hatred in my heart for those who have wronged me.
	Unfulfilled	My life does not hold meaning, and/or I am not content with my life.
	Unimportant	I am not important to others, and/or I am of little or no priority.
	Unknown	I'm afraid to move forward because the outcome is uncertain, and/or if I am not prepared, then I won't feel secure.
	Unloved	Others do not love me, and/or my spouse or others have no affection, care, or desire for me.
	Unwanted	I am not desirable, and/or people are in relationships with me out of duty or obligation.
	Used	I have been taken advantage of and not compensated for my help.
	Weak	When push comes to shove, I will always lose because I am not strong enough.
	Worried	Life will not go well for me, and/or bad things will happen to me or those I care about.
	Worthless	My value and worth are not recognized; I feel cheapened, less than, or devalued in relationships; and/or I have little or no value to others.
	Other:	
	Other:	

Check all the ways you have reacted to hurts over time. Then, place a star next to the top three to five that seem consistent for you.

X	Reactions to Hurt	Explanation
	Abdicate	You give away or deny your authority and/or responsibility.
	Act Out	You engage in negative behaviors like drug or alcohol abuse, extramarital affairs, excessive shopping, or overeating.
	Anger or Rage	You display strong feelings of displeasure or violent and uncontrolled emotions.
	Arrogance	You posture yourself as superior, better than, or wiser than others.
	Avoidance	You participate in activities to avoid others or certain topics.
	Belittle	You devalue or dishonor someone with words or actions, and/or you call other people names, use insults, ridicule, or mock them.
	Blame	You place responsibility on others, not accepting fault; you're convinced the problem is someone else's fault
	Broadcast	You share your problems and concerns with people outside of your marriage or outside of the people involved.
	Care Take	You regularly take on the burdens of others; you find it hard to rest until everyone around you is provided for; and/or you "over-function" by taking on the details, tasks, and responsibility of others.
	Catastrophize	You use dramatic, exaggerated expressions to depict that the hurt was worse than it really was.
	Clinginess	You develop a strong emotional attachment or dependence to your spouse or others, and/or you tightly hold onto other people.

	Complain	You readily express unhappiness.
	Control	You hold back, restrain, oppress, or dominate other people; you "rule over" them; and/or you talk over or prevent others from having a chance to explain their position, opinions, or feelings.
	Criticize	You find and verbalize fault in others, and/or you bring up what is wrong and focus on negative aspects of others.
	Cross-Complain	You often meet others' complaints (or criticisms) with an immediate complaint of your own.
	Defensiveness	Instead of listening, you defend yourself by providing an explanation, and/or you make excuses for your actions.
	Demand	You try to force others to do something, usually with an implied threat of punishment if they refuse.
	Denial	You ignore the truth or reality and refuse to admit it.
	Dishonesty	You lie about, fail to reveal, and give false impressions of your thoughts, feelings, habits, likes, dislikes, personal history, daily activities, or plans for the future.
	Earn-It Mode	You try to do more to earn others' love and care.
	Escalate	Your emotions spiral out of control, and/or you argue, raise your voice, or fly into a rage.
	Right/Wrong	You argue about who is right and who is wrong, and/or you debate whose position is the correct one.
	Righteous Indignation	You believe that you deserve to be angry, resentful, or annoyed with others because of what they did.
	Righteousness	You make it a moral issue by arguing about issues of morality or righteousness.
	Sarcasm	You use negative or hostile humor, hurtful words, belittling comments, cutting remarks, or demeaning statements.

	Self-Abandon	You desert or neglect yourself, and/or you take care of everyone except yourself.
	Self-Deprecate	You run yourself down or become very critical of yourself.
	Selfishness	You are concerned with your interests, feelings, wants, or desires while disregarding or paying little heed to those of others.
	Shut Down	You emotionally detach yourself and close your heart towards others, you become numb, and/or you become devoid of emotion.
	Stonewall	You put up walls and stop responding to others, and/or you refuse to share or show any emotion.
	Strike-Out	You lash out in anger and/or become verbally or physically aggressive or abusive.
	Stubborn	You will not budge from your position, and/or you become inflexible or persistent.
	Tantrums	You have fits of bad temper, and/or you become irritable, crabby, or grumpy.
	Vent	You emotionally "vomit," unload, or dump on others.
	Withdraw	You pull out of arguments when they become too much; once you pull out, you rarely, if ever, revisit the conflict; and/or you become distant, sulk, or use the silent treatment.
	Withhold	You hold back your affections, feelings, sexual intimacy, or love from others.
	Yes, But...	You start out agreeing (yes), but then you end up disagreeing (but).
	Other:	
	Other:	

Check all the needs you have felt at some time as a result of your hurts. Then, place a star next to the top three to five that seem consistent for you.

X	Needs Resulting from Hurts	What That Feeling Sounds Like
	Acceptance	I want to be warmly received for who I am without conditions.
	Accurately Portrayed	I want to be seen correctly, and/or I want my peers to represent me in a true and accurate manner.
	Adequate	I want to feel like I measure up and am good enough.
	Affection	I want to feel fondness and warmth.
	Appreciation	I want what I do to be noticed, valued, and acknowledged.
	Approval	I want to be liked and accepted.
	Assistance	I want a helpmate, and/or I want help, support, backing, and assistance from others.
	Attention	I want to be noticed and attended to.
	Care	I want to know that others feel concern for me and are interested in my wellbeing.
	Comfort	I want to feel a sense of wellbeing.
	Commitment	I want to have unconditional security in relationships.
	Companionship	I want to enjoy spending time with others and want them to feel the same with me.
	Competence	I want to have skills and abilities that bring success.
	Connection	I want to feel close to others.
	Direction	I want to feel guided by something larger than myself.
	Forgiveness	I want to be released from the wrongs I have committed.
	Friends	I want relationships that move beyond the surface level.
	Grace	I want to handle hardships well.

	Hope	I want to feel excited for what's ahead.
	Important	I want to feel relevant, significant, and of high priority to others.
	Intimacy/ Vulnerability	I want to open my heart and not have walls with others, and/or I want to feel a deep closeness and connection with others.
	Joy	I want to feel lasting satisfaction and happiness.
	Knowledge	I want to understand and be understood.
	Love	I want to be deeply loved, and/or I want to know that others think of me as lovable.
	Partnership	I want to feel like I am not on my own.
	Passion	I want excitement, fascination, intrigue, and adventure.
	Patience	I want to be present and grateful in each moment.
	Peacefulness	I want calmness, serenity, and tranquility.
	Power	I want to impact and influence others, and/or I want to know that what I do makes a difference.
	Respect	I want to be admired and esteemed.
	Safety	I want to feel protected and secure.
	Self-Determination	I want to have independence and free will.
	Significance	I want to have meaning and purpose.
	Strength	I want the confidence to know that I can do all things through Christ.
	Success	I want to experience a sense of achievement and accomplishment.
	Support	I want others to be on my side.
	To Forget	I want the bad memories to fade.
	Trust	I want to have faith in others and know they are reliable.
	Understanding	I want to be known and understood at a deep level.
	Useful	I want to contribute something valuable to others.

Validation	I want to feel valued for who I am, what I think, and how I feel.	
Valued	I want to feel honored and treasured.	
Wanted	I want to be sought after, and/or I want to be desirable.	
Other:		
Other:		

Hurt and Fear Cycle of Discontent

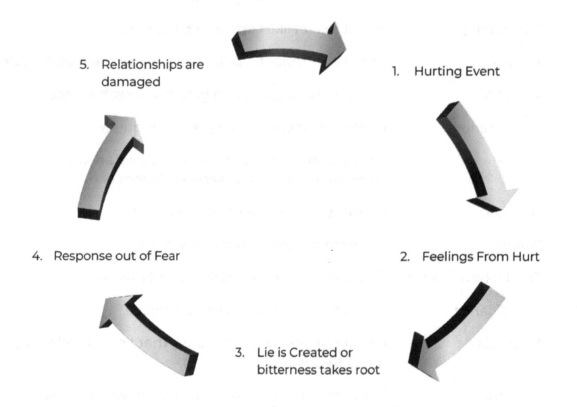

5. Relationships are damaged

1. Hurting Event

4. Response out of Fear

2. Feelings From Hurt

3. Lie is Created or bitterness takes root

Replace the lie with a promise of God and control the only thing you can: your response, with God fulfilling your needs instead of people. Realize your needs and the needs of others, and then chose to respond in a way that serves those needs, breaking the cycle.

Remember, we are trying to align mind and heart in the pursuit of peace and joy. Here are some Bible verses to reinforce truth while managing feelings. The first two here are pivotal! We have also included twenty memory-verse cards for you in the appendix of this workbook. Those verses directly coincide with the program materials and can ensure that you don't find yourself in the cycle of unrest again, if you will commit them to memory.

✦ Romans 12:2: "Do not conform to the pattern of this world, but be transformed by the renewing of your mind. Then you will be able to test and approve what God's will is—his good, pleasing and perfect will."

✦ Proverbs 4:23: "Above all else, guard your heart, for everything you do flows from it."

Afraid	Psalms 27:1, Psalms 56:3, John 4:18
Angry	Ecclesiastes 7:9, James 1:19-20, Psalms 4:4, Matthew 5:22
Anxious	Matthew 6:25-28, Philippians 4:6-7, 1 Peter 5:6-7
Confused	Proverbs 20:24, James 1:5, 1 Corinthians 13:12
Depressed	Psalms 103:2-5, Psalms 43:5, Isaiah 53:4
Discouraged	Psalms 51:10, Psalms 33:22, 2 Corinthians 3:12
Embarrassed	Isaiah 44:22, Psalms 25:3, Luke 6:26
Forsaken	Romans 14:7, John 14:18, Psalms 118:8
Frustrated	Isaiah 40:29, Romans 15:4, James 1:2-3
Guilty	Psalms 32:5, Isaiah 1:18, 1 Corinthians 6:1
Hurt	2 Timothy 4:18, Romans 8:18, Romans 5:3-4
Like Giving Up	Psalms 62:5, Psalms 33:22, Romans 15:13, 2 Thessalonians 2:16-17
Lonely	James 4:8, Psalms 145:18, Matthew 26:41

Sad	Psalms 118:24, John 17:13, Psalms 119:28
Tempted	1 Corinthians 10:13, James 1:13-14, Matthew 26:41
Threatened	Psalms 145:20, Philippians 1:27-28, Hebrews 13:6
Troubled	Psalms 112:7, Psalms 30:11-12, Psalms 43:5, James 5:13
Unforgiving	Matthew 6:14-15, Mark 11:25, 1 Corinthians 13:5, Ephesians 4:31-32
Unfulfilled	John 6:35, Psalms 145:16, John 10:10
Used	Psalms 22:24, Isaiah 53:3, 1 Peter 2:20
Weak	2 Corinthians 12:9, Isaiah 40:31, Philippians 4:13
Worried	1 Peter 5:7, Philippians 4:6-7, Luke 12:25-26

Hope and Peace From the Inside Out

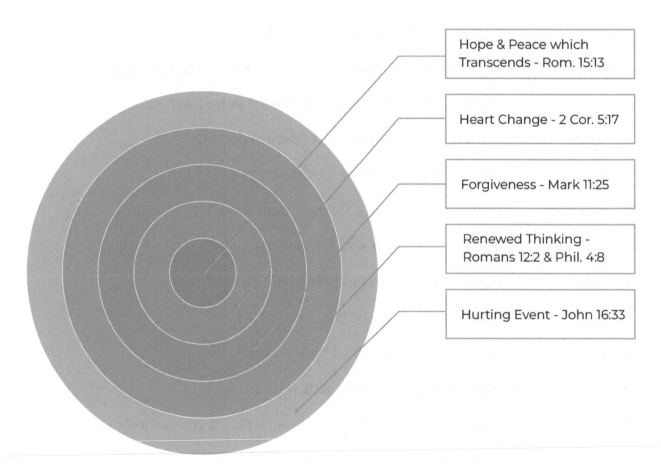

Be encouraged: scar tissue is actually stronger than regular tissue.

Remember, we are here to pursue two objectives:

1. _____—fears overcome by God's promises.

2. _____—hurts surrendered to forgiveness.

Luke 6:45: "A good man brings good things out of the good stored up in his heart, and an evil man brings evil things out of the evil stored up in his heart. For the mouth speaks what the heart is full of."

The recipe for hope and peace consists of two character traits of spiritual maturity—_____ and _____. Both require a decision that precedes feelings. Feelings will follow. Some are so tired that they will surrender right away and have peace, but some will have to rely on consistent obedience until the walls come down. All will have to rely on obedience thereafter to avoid finding themselves in a cycle of discontent again.

1. **Continual Surrender:** counterintuitive to everything the world tells us.

2. **Relentless Obedience:** the decisions are easy if we truly believe what we say we believe.

How do we honor God in our actions?

Live to please God and only God. Be obedient to God's calling for you, not selfish ambitions or pleasing others. This is the "why" behind making these changes, and it's imperative if we are to reach spiritual maturity and have a chance at true joy and lasting peace.

Aligning mind and heart, and relentlessly obeying will develop a Christ-like character. Character change is what we are after, not simply personality change, habit change, or relationship change. We cannot be simultaneously filled with the Holy Spirit and with bitterness and/or fear. Transcending peace will come when the mind and heart are aligned with Christ.

Now, let's take an assessment to determine your personality type according to the DiSC® profile. This assessment will help us better understand your behaviors and discuss how they might help or hinder your efforts to be renewed and transformed moving forward.

The DiSC® is a personal assessment tool that measures your personality and behavioral style. DiSC profiles describe human behavior in various situations, such as how you respond to challenges, how you influence others, your preferred pace, and how you respond to rules and procedures.

There are a few guidelines to follow when obtaining your personality profile:

Be honest: Do not censor your answers. Your first reply is your most accurate.

Pick your environment: Compartmentalizing life is a typical tendency, meaning you may act one way at work, one way at home, and one way at church. For consistency, mentally choose the environment in which you spend the majority of your time.

Rate yourself using one of the following:

Never: This is never true for me, or this never applies to me.

Rarely: This is rarely true for me, or this rarely applies to me.

Sometimes: This is sometimes true for me, or this sometimes applies to me.

Often: This is often true for me, or this often applies to me.

Always: This is always true for me, or this always applies to me.

**Try to stay away from "Sometimes," as this can alter receiving the most accurate results.

Record your results on the My Story page in the appendix of this workbook, so we can have further discussion around it.

SPIRITUAL GIFTS QUESTIONS

Next, let's complete the Spiritual Gifts assessment to identify the gifts that God has blessed you with, so you can be fulfilled as you contribute to the body of Christ.

We will guide you through the directions of completing this Spiritual Gifts assessment.

1.	I like organizing events.
2.	I enjoy starting new things.
3.	I love working with my hands.
4.	I can tell when someone is insincere.
5.	I pray for lost and unchurched people daily.
6.	Encouraging others is a high priority in my life.
7.	Believing God for my daily needs is important to me
8.	Helping others through my finances is extremely important to me.
9.	I look for opportunities to pray for the sick.
10.	I enjoy doing the little things that others do not.
11.	Having people over to my house is something I do often.
12.	Spending hours in prayer for other people is very enjoyable to me.

13.	Education is very important to me.
14.	I tend to motivate others to get involved.
15.	My heart hurts when I see others hurting.
16.	I believe God will use me to enact His miracles.
17.	I enjoy sharing Jesus with other people in other nations.
18.	I've devoted a lot of time to mastering my voice and/or instrument.
19.	Caring for the hurting is the most important thing in my eyes.
20.	The willful sin of others really aggravates me.
21.	I enjoy serving behind the scenes.
22.	I like creating outlines of the Bible.
23.	God has used me to interpret a heavenly language.
24.	I enjoy the book of Proverbs more than any other book in the Bible.
25.	I am passionate about managing the details.
26.	I prefer to start/begin new projects.
27.	I consider myself a craftsman or craftswoman.
28.	I sense when situations are unhealthy.
29.	I am greatly concerned about seeing the lost saved.
30.	I try to come across loving and caring.
31.	Asking God for a list of big things is exciting to me.
32.	I find ways to give offerings above my tithe.
33.	I believe miraculous healing is for this day and age.
34.	Helping others is one of my highest achievements.
35.	Having a welcoming home is important to me.
36.	I always pray for situations and leaders in the world.
37.	People seek me out to learn more about God.
38.	I prefer to take the lead whenever necessary.
39.	I'm very sensitive to sad stories.

40. Miracles often happen when I'm nearby.

41. Living in another country to share the love of Jesus is exciting to me.

42. I desire to serve the church through worship.

43. I enjoy connecting, caring for, and coaching others.

44. Confronting someone with sin in their life is not hard.

45. It bothers me when people sit around and do nothing.

46. I share Biblical truth with others in hopes of their personal growth

47. I pray in tongues daily.

48. When I study scripture God gives me unique insights.

49. Creating a to-do list is easy and enjoyable for me.

50. I am attracted to ministries that start new churches.

51. Building something with my hands is very rewarding to me.

52. I can pinpoint issues or problems before others.

53. I enjoy sharing Christ with a total stranger.

54. I look for ways to be an encouragement to other people.

55. I trust that God has my back in every situation.

56. Making more money means that I can give more.

57. God has used me to bring healing to those who are sick.

58. Being a part of the process is fulfilling to me.

59. I tend to make total strangers feel at home.

60. People often describe me as a prayer warrior.

61. I enjoy knowing biblical details and helping others to understand.

62. I delegate responsibilities to accomplish tasks.

63. I am motivated to help those who are less fortunate.

64. I have a constant desire to see God's miraculous power.

65. I focus a lot on reaching the world for Christ.

66. I am most excited leading others in vocal or instrumental worship.

67.	I enjoy walking with someone during their difficult situations.
68.	I enjoy hearing passionate and clear preaching of the truth.
69.	I like to do small things that others pass over.
70.	I prefer to teach the Bible topically rather than verse by verse.
71.	Praying in the Spirit is encouraging and important to me.
72.	When faced with hard times, I tend to make wise decisions and choices.

SPIRITUAL GIFTS RATINGS

1 = Almost Never,   2 = Seldom,   3 = Sometimes,   4 = Frequently,   5 = Almost Always

TOTAL

1. ____	25. ____	48. ____	_____	A. _____
2. ____	26. ____	50. ____	_____	B. _____
3. ____	27. ____	51. ____	_____	C. _____
4. ____	28. ____	52. ____	_____	D. _____
5. ____	29. ____	53. ____	_____	E. _____
6. ____	30. ____	54. ____	_____	F. _____
7. ____	31. ____	55. ____	_____	G. _____
8. ____	32. ____	56. ____	_____	H. _____
9. ____	33. ____	57. ____	_____	I. _____
10. ____	34. ____	58. ____	_____	J. _____
11. ____	35. ____	59. ____	_____	K. _____
12. ____	36. ____	60. ____	_____	L. _____
13. ____	37. ____	61. ____	_____	M. _____
14. ____	38. ____	62. ____	_____	N. _____
15. ____	39. ____	63. ____	_____	O. _____
16. ____	40. ____	64. ____	_____	P. _____
17. ____	41. ____	65. ____	_____	Q. _____
18. ____	42. ____	66. ____	_____	R. _____
19. ____	43. ____	67. ____	_____	S. _____
20. ____	44. ____	68. ____	_____	T. _____
21. ____	45. ____	69. ____	_____	U. _____
22. ____	46. ____	70. ____	_____	V. _____
23. ____	47. ____	71. ____	_____	W. _____
24. ____	48. ____	72. ____	_____	X. _____

GIFT DEFINITIONS AND SCRIPTURE REFERENCES

The following contains definitions of the spiritual gifts. While not meant to be dogmatic or final, these definitions and supporting scriptures do correspond to characteristics of the gifts as expressed in the gifts questionnaire.

A. ADMINISTRATION

The gift of administration is the divine strength or ability to organize multiple tasks and groups of people to accomplish these tasks. (Luke 14:28-30; Acts 6: 1-7; 1 Corinthians 12:28)

B. APOSTLESHIP

The gift of apostleship is the divine strength or ability to pioneer new churches and ministries through planting, overseeing, and training. (Acts 15:22-35; 1 Corinthians 12:28; 2 Corinthians 12:12; Galatians 2:7-10; Ephesians 4:11-14)

C. CRAFTSMANSHIP

The gift of craftsmanship is the divine strength or ability to plan, build, and work with your hands in construction environments to accomplish multiple ministry applications. (Exodus 30:22, 31 :3-11; 2 Chronicles 34:9-13; Acts 18:2-3)

D. DISCERNMENT

The gift of discernment is the divine strength or ability to spiritually identify falsehood and to distinguish between right and wrong motives and situations. (Matthew 16:21-23; Acts 5:1-11, 16: 16-18; 1 Corinthians 12:10; 1 John 4: 1-6)

E. EVANGELISM

The gift of evangelism is the divine strength or ability to help non-Christians take the necessary steps to becoming a born-again Christian. (Acts 8:5-6, 8:26-40, 14:21, 21:8; Ephesians 4:11-14)

F. EXHORTATION

The gift of exhortation is the divine strength or ability to encourage others through the written or spoken word and Biblical truth. (Acts 14:22; Romans 12:8; 1 Timothy 4:13; Hebrews 10:24-25)

G. FAITH

The gift of faith is the divine strength or ability to believe in God for unseen supernatural results in every arena of life. (Acts 11 :22-24; Romans 4:18-21; 1 Corinthians 12:9; Hebrews 11)

H GIVING

The gift of giving is the divine strength or ability to produce wealth and to give by tithes and offerings for the purpose of advancing the Kingdom of God on Earth. (Mark 12:41-44; Romans 12:8; 2 Corinthians 8:1-7, 9:2-7)

I. HEALING

The gift of healing is the divine strength or ability to act as an intermediary in faith, prayer, and by the laying-on of hands for the healing of physical and mental illnesses. (Acts 3:1-10, 9:32-35, 28:7-10; 1 Corinthians 12:9, 28)

J. HELPS

The gift of helps is the divine strength or ability to work in a supportive role for the accomplishment of tasks in Christian ministry. (Mark 15:40-41; Acts 9:36; Romans 16:1-2; 1 Corinthians 12:28)

K. HOSPITALITY

The gift of hospitality is the divine strength or ability to create warm, welcoming environments for others in places such as your home, office, or church. (Acts 16:14-15; Romans 12:13, 16:23; Hebrews 13:1-2; 1 Peter 4:9)

L. INTERCESSION

The gift of intercession is the divine strength or ability to stand in the gap in prayer for someone, something, or someplace, believing for profound results. (Hebrews 7:25; Colossians 1:9-12, 4:12-13; James 5:14-16)

M. KNOWLEDGE

The gift of knowledge is the divine strength or ability to understand and bring clarity to situations and circumstances often accompanied by a word from God. (Acts 5:1-11; 1 Corinthians 12:8; Colossians 2:2-3)

N. LEADERSHIP

The gift of leadership is the divine strength or ability to influence people at their level while directing and focusing them on the big picture, vision, or idea. (Romans 12:8; 1 Timothy 3:1-13, 5:17; Hebrews 13:17)

O. MERCY

The gift of mercy is the divine strength or ability to feel empathy and to care for those who are hurting in any way. (Matthew 9:35-36; Mark 9:41; Romans 12:8; 1 Thessalonians 5:14)

P. MIRACLES

The gift of miracles is the divine strength or ability to alter the natural outcomes of life in a supernatural way through prayer, faith, and divine direction. (Acts 9:36-42, 19:11-12, 20:7-12; Romans 15:18-19; 1 Corinthians 12:10, 28)

Q. MISSIONARY

The gift of missions is the divine strength or ability to reach others outside of your culture and nationality, while in most cases living in that culture or nation. (Acts 8:4, 13:2-3, 22:21; Romans 10:15)

R. MUSIC/ WORSHIP

The gift of music/worship is the divine strength or ability to sing, dance, or play an instrument primarily for the purpose of helping others worship God. (Deuteronomy 31:22; 1 Samuel 16:16; 1 Chronicles 16:41-42; 2 Chronicles 5:12-13, 34:12; Psalm 150)

S. PASTOR/SHEPHERD

The gift of pastor/shepherd is the divine strength or ability to care for the personal needs of others by nurturing and mending life issues. (John 10:1-18; Ephesians 4:11-14; 1 Timothy 3:1-7; 1 Peter 5:1-3)

T. PROPHECY

The gift of prophecy is the divine strength or ability to speak boldly and bring clarity to scriptural and doctrinal truth, in some cases foretelling God's plan. (Acts 2:37-40, 7:51-53, 26:24-29; 1 Corinthians 14: 1-4; 1 Thessalonians 1:5)

U. SERVICE

The gift of serving is the divine strength or ability to do small or great tasks in working for the overall good of the body of Christ. (Acts 6:1-7; Romans 12:7; Galatians 6:10; 1 Timothy 1:16-18; Titus 3:14)

V. TEACHING

The gift of teaching is the divine strength or ability to study and learn from the Scriptures primarily to bring understanding and depth to other Christians. (Acts 18:24-28, 20:20-21; 1 Corinthians 12:28; Ephesians 4:11-14)

W. TONGUES (and Interpretation)

The gift of tongues is the divine strength or ability to pray in a heavenly language to encourage your spirit and to commune with God. The gift of tongues is often accompanied by interpretation and should be used appropriately. (Acts 2:1-13; 1 Corinthians 12:10, 14:1-14)

X. WISDOM

The gift of wisdom is the divine strength or ability to apply the truths of Scripture in a practical way, producing the fruitful outcome and character of Jesus Christ. (Acts 6:3, 10; 1 Corinthians 2:6-13, 12:8)

Record your top three results on the My Story page in the appendix of this workbook, so we can have further discussion around it.

Discover Your Love Language

Finally, let's complete the 5 Love Languages assessment to see how you best relate love to others and how you best receive love from others as well.

It is within your love language that
you relate to and understand others best.

REFLECTION QUESTIONS

1. Which of your personality assessment results is most surprising and why?

2. Which of your spiritual gifts assessment results is most surprising to you?

3. Do you think your love language often differs from others?

CHAPTER 4

HOW YOUR STORY FITS IN GOD'S STORY

Everything we've done to this point in the program has been intended for one purpose. You now have everything you need in order to have an authentic experience and conversation with God. The next step is to unplug from distractions and spend a few hours alone with Him. On our retreats, this might be a hike through some trails or finding a quiet place by the lake to sit still. Others have scheduled a dinner date at home alone with Him or gone away for the weekend uninterrupted.

This is an opportunity to look back at what has shaped your story to this point and reconcile any assumptions, let go of the hurts, forgive those who have hurt you, replace some lies and fears with the truths of God's word, commit or recommit to a decision to live for Christ, and explore what God may have for the next chapters of your story. Let this be a day in your journey of faith that will be remembered and provide encouragement.

Preparing for Your Time with God

_____: even Jesus needed it. Church as a group twice per month is not enough to sustain a relationship with God, so it's important to have one-on-one time as well.

God is the author of our story, and therefore, He is the only one who can rewrite it. If you are not hearing from Him, three barriers may be in the way of His ability to connect with you: _____, _____, and/or _____. Consider whether any of these are holding you back.

The goal is always to have a transformed mind and heart. One without the other is not effective. Pray in the days leading up to your time with God for a willing, humble, and surrendered mind and heart.

✦ Remove distractions.

✦ Ask God to reveal anything that is keeping you from Him.

✦ Ask God to reveal areas of control.

✦ Seek Him, meditate on Him, and praise Him.

✦ Ask and listen.

✦ Make room by allowing silence.

✦ Identify and rebuke disruption.

✦ Bring the tools from the Transcend program.

  ▪ Bible

  ▪ Notes

  ▪ My Story results page

  ▪ Any scripture references

  ▪ Salvation resource

  ▪ Forgiveness resource

  ▪ Self-acceptance and victory over fears/lies resource

  ▪ Your will, not mine resource

  ▪ Any dreams, desires, or passions that you need to seek His will about

✦ Consider that the Bible begins and ends with God speaking to someone.

✦ Ask God to speak to you through his word, the Holy Spirit, by writing out a prayer or journal note.

✦ Be prepared for Him to answer.

✦ Be attentive to everything.

✦ Be okay with asking for confirmation.

✦ Take the time to enjoy His presence.

✦ Commit to connecting with Him more regularly.

PRAYER FOR QUIET TIME WITH GOD

"Search me, God, and know my heart; test me and know my anxious thoughts. See if there is any offensive way in me, and lead me in the way everlasting" (Psalms 139:23-24).

The Bible gives us the message, or gospel, of how to be saved. By this, we mean how to be forgiven for our sins and gain eternal life. Summarized below are the steps for salvation as presented in the Bible. I invite you to receive Christ as your Savior.

1. **Agree**

   a. Agree in your heart with God that you are a sinner in need of His salvation, "for all have sinned and fall short of the glory of God" (Romans 3:23).

2. **Know**

   a. Know in your heart that there is a penalty to your sin, "for the wages of sin is death" (Romans 6:23).

3. **Believe**

   a. Believe in your heart that Christ died on the cross and rose from the dead to pay the penalty for your sins and give you eternal life.

   b. "But God demonstrates his own love for us in this: While we were still sinners, Christ died for us" (Romans 5:8).

   c. "All are justified freely by his grace through the redemption that came by Christ Jesus" (Romans 3:24).

   d. "For God so loved the world that he gave his one and only Son, that whoever believes in him shall not perish but have eternal life" (John 3:16).

   e. "But the gift of God is eternal life in Christ Jesus our Lord" (Romans 6:23).

4. **Ask**

   a. By faith, pray to God. Tell Him you believe the above in your heart, and ask Him to save you through Jesus Christ. Remember that God is more concerned with the attitude of your heart rather than your exact words.

   b. "For it is by grace you have been saved, through faith—and this is not from yourselves, it is the gift of God—not by works, so that no one can boast" (Ephesians 2:8-9).

   c. "If you declare with your mouth, 'Jesus is Lord,' and believe in your heart that God raised him from the dead, you shall be saved. For it is with your heart that you believe and are justified, and it is with your mouth that you profess your faith and are saved" (Romans 10:9-10).

   d. "Here I am! I stand at the door and knock. If anyone hears my voice and opens the door, I will come in and eat with that person, and they with me" (Revelation 3:20).

   e. "Yet to all who did receive him, to those who believed in his name, he gave the right to become children of God—children born not of natural descent, nor of human decision or a husband's will, but born of God" (John 1:12-13).

5. **Receive**

   a. The following is a suggested prayer:

   b. Heavenly Father, I admit to you that I am a sinner in need of your salvation. I believe that Christ died on the cross and rose from the dead to pay for my sins and give me eternal life. I believe that only through Christ can I be saved. I ask for and accept by faith your free gift of salvation. Please come into my heart and be my Savior and Lord. Thank you for doing so. In Jesus' name, Amen!

Remember: forgiveness is simply releasing the debt and justice to God where it belongs. This is an act of your will which starts with a decision. The feelings will follow as you allow the Holy Spirit to minister to you in these moments.

Remember: forgiveness is not justifying, condoning, understanding, excusing, trivializing, forgetting, saying it's okay, reconciling, denying the hurt, liking that person, or letting your guard down. It's not letting them off the hook altogether; it's letting them off *your* hook and simply leaving them on God's hook. It's not even asking God to forgive them.

Read: Ephesians 4:31-32 and Matthew 6:14-15.

 Prayer of Forgiveness

Lord, there are some unhealthy feelings from the hurting events and fears in my life that I need to lay down before you at the cross today. There are also some lies that I came to believe as a result of these hurts and fears which I need your help in overcoming. I am simply not strong enough to carry these burdens any further, and I realize now that I was never meant to. Father in heaven, I confess these feelings of _____ to you and ask that you take them from me and heal me in this very moment. I pray for each of the people by name, _____, who took part in these hurts, and release the burden of debt I feel they may owe back to you where it belongs. *(Note: name each person and say, "Because I am forgiven in Christ, I forgive you and unconditionally release you from the hurts.")* Father, I recognize that it is not up to me to judge them, and I confess that I am also sinfully broken and in need of your grace. I choose to forgive each of them unconditionally, and I wish them well in their journeys to know You and achieve peace because I am forgiven and accepted by you through Christ Jesus. Lord, please forgive me for any hurt that I may have caused others out of my own pain, and help me walk in forgiveness and grace each day forward. Father, I receive your unconditional love and acceptance in place of these hurts, and I trust that you will meet all of my needs as I seek you wholeheartedly. I claim victory over the enemy and take back any ground that he gained in my life to this point. Father, please walk in step with me in the days to come, as I seek to honor You as a follower of Christ. Amen!

Remember: you don't have to carry the burden of forgiving yourself. Only God can forgive you, and He already has. Receive His forgiveness and accept your faults. Your brokenness is made perfect in Christ! After all, your faults are part of your story and have led you to this very moment, and that is what God desires most.

Remember: just as in kintsugi, beauty can come from our brokenness.

Read: Romans 8:15, Hebrews 13:5-6, and 1 John 4:18.

 Prayer of Victory Over Fears

Father, I humbly approach You in Your throne room and kneel before You because You alone are worthy. God, I am a sinner in need of Your grace, and I thank You for choosing me in light of this. I acknowledge my brokenness and recognize now that the lies which stemmed from these events have caused separation from You until now. Thank You for not defining me by these lies or my past mistakes. I understand that You are the God who makes good of all things, and I pray that You will do just that with me, Lord. Use my story, all of it, to keep me reliant on You and help me reflect Your light to the world around me. I choose to stand on the truths found in Your word which demolish the lies of the enemy. Lord, some of the lies that I have come to believe are:

_____ .

Father, please highlight the very things which have kept me from You so that others might see Your glory and take a step towards You as a result. Let me be the change in my family, my work, my friendships, the church, and wherever else You lead me. I claim victory over the guilt and shame that the enemy whispers in my ear, the things people have said to me, and the generational patterns of my family and instead find redemption through Christ Jesus over all of it. I surrender my life to You in this moment and pray that You fill me with Your Holy Spirit so I can walk in victory for all my days. Amen!

Remember: God's plan is way better than anything you can possibly dream up. Seek Him, and seek His plan.

Read: Matthew 6:33, Romans 8:28, Jeremiah 29:12-13, Proverbs 3:5-6

Prayer to Seek God's Will

Heavenly Father, I thank You for this very moment in Your presence, and I quiet my mind and heart so that I might hear Your voice more clearly. Will You make certain to me the passions You have placed on my heart that would honor You most and bring fulfillment to Your plan for my life? I confess that I try to take the reins of life into my own hands without first coming to You, and I ask Your forgiveness for this, Lord. I commit to surrendering my future plans to You and ask that You would bless them if they are in line with Your will. If they are not, will You open my mind and heart to receive Your will for my life, open the doors to pursue it, and close those doors which lead me away from it? Father, I know that Your will for me is far better than anything I could dream of, and I commit to be the light wherever You lead me. Help me be the best Christ-follower, wife/husband, mother/father, daughter/son, sister/brother, worker/boss, etc. possible. Transform my mind and purify my heart so that I can now respond in ways that stand out in this world and honor You. Amen!

REFLECTION QUESTIONS

1. What is holding you back from connecting with Him?

2. What will you do to connect with Him deeply and more frequently?

3. How will you forgive others for their wrongs going forward?

CHAPTER 5

YOUR NEXT AND BEST CHAPTERS

From what we say to how we respond each moment, we make numerous decisions every day. In fact, it's estimated that we make around 35,000 decisions per day. That's one approximately every 2.5 seconds of our waking hours. Imagine how far off we can find ourselves at the end of a day with only a few poor choices. Now imagine where we might be after a lifetime. We are all only one bad decision away from disaster at any point. We are also only one decision of surrender away from redemption in Christ.

Step off the ledge and test Him moving forward. Your gifts of time, talent, and treasure should be considered as you make a plan to leverage your resources now as a "knower." Make a plan that includes discipline, accountability partners, and resources pertaining to your physical, mental and spiritual health.

See other people and circumstances through the lens of Jesus. Be positive, blessing-focused, humble, and not judgmental. Above all, remember to love _____; love _____.

This cannot be a halfhearted commitment of _____. We cannot be lukewarm in our faith. If we are, we will call "Lord, Lord," and He will say, "I don't know you."

The only thing that can stand in your way from here forward is pride.

REFLECTION QUESTION

1. What is one way that you experienced God going beyond surface level with you during this time?

2. How do we make the best decision each time?

3. How will you make a difference going forward?

Don't get drawn into surface-level faith again. Remember the differences:

Surface-Level Faith	Spirit-Driven Faith
Built on assumptions	Built on the Bible
Box-checking mentality	Grace mentality
Based on self-works	Based on humbly serving God and others
Defined by people	Defined by the life of Christ
Questionable in hard times	Unshakable
Shaped by the world	Shaped by the Holy Spirit through word, grace, testimony, and prayer
Produces pride	Produces fruit of the spirit
Damages God's kingdom	Builds God's kingdom
Lukewarm	On fire for God
Worships self/others/stuff	Worships one God through Jesus with the Holy Spirit
Cycle of discontent	Mind, heart, and spirit aligned for peace and joy

Your Next Chapter

What has the Holy Spirit convinced you of during this time regarding the improvement of your *physical* health? _____

_____

_____

_____

_____

_____

_____

What has the Holy Spirit convinced you of during this time regarding the improvement of your *mental* health? _____

_____

_____

_____

_____

_____

What has the Holy Spirit convinced you of during this time regarding the improvement of your *spiritual* health? _____

_____

_____

_____

_____

_____

Do you have the right support systems in place to accomplish these things? ___

_____

Consistent quiet time with God: _____

_____

A church to serve with and tithe through: _____

_____

Small group of like-minded believers to do life with: _____

_____

Mentor to hold you accountable: _____

_____

Primary care physician to help manage physical health: _____

_____

Counselor/therapist for any additional needs in managing trauma: _____

_____

Resources to grow further: A plan to use your spiritual gifts for His glory: _____

_____

Encouragement for the Next Chapter

- ✦ **Forgiveness is not a one-time event, but a lifestyle**. - Matthew 18:21-22

- ✦ **Healing is not a one-time event, but a process**. - Philippians 1:6, 2 Corinthians 3:18

- ✦ **God wants you to live your live in health and wholeness**. - 3 John 1:2, Psalm 147:3, Malachi 4:2

- ✦ **Be dependent on the Holy Spirit every day.** - Zechariah 4:6, John 16:13, John 14:26

- ✦ **Casting your cares on the Lord is a daily process.** - 1 Peter 5:7-9

- ✦ **Take every thought captive.** - 2 Corinthians 10:4-5, Philippians 4:8, Romans 12:2

- ✦ **Maintain an attitude of gratitude.** - 1 Thessalonians 5:18, Psalm 100:4, 1 Chronicles 16:34, Psalm 50:23

- ✦ **There is power in your words.** - Proverbs 18:20-21, Proverbs 21:23, Proverbs 18:7

- ✦ **There is power in speaking God's word.** - Isaiah 55:11, Matthew 5:23-24

- ✦ **You can overcome and resist temptation.** - 1 Corinthians 10:13, James 1:14, Galatians 5:16, James 4:7, Matthew 6:13

- ✦ **Be careful who you keep company with** - 1 Corinthians 15:33 (AMP), Proverbs 13:20, Proverbs 14:7

- ✦ **You can have hope enduring adversity and trials**. - James 1:2-3, James 1:12

- ✦ **You can have peace in the midst of storms.** - Isaiah 26:3, John 14:27, John 16:33

- ✦ **You can have freedom from all fear.** - Psalm 34:4, 2 Timothy 1:7

- ✦ **God gives you the promise of sleep.** - Proverbs 3:24, Psalm 4:8, Psalm 127:2

- ✦ **You can achieve victory through spiritual warfare.** - 2 Chronicles 20:15b, Deuteronomy 20:4, 1 Corinthians 15:57, Isaiah 41:13

- ✦ **Put the past behind you.** - Philippians 3:12-14, Mark 5:1-20

- ✦ **Put into practice what you've learned.** - Philippians 4:9

- ✦ **God gives you the promise of restoration.** - Psalm 23:3, Joel 2:25a, Revelation 21:5

- ✦ **God has a plan for your life.** - Jeremiah 29:11

Here are a few additional parting encouragements through scripture:

- ✦ 1 Thessalonians 5:16-18: "Rejoice always, pray continually, give thanks in all circumstances; for this is God's will for you in Christ Jesus."

- ✦ Romans 8:28: "And we know that in all things God works for the good of those who love him, who have been called according to his purpose."

- ✦ Romans 12:12: "Be joyful in hope, patient in affliction, faithful in prayer."

- ✦ Colossians 3:12-15: "Therefore, as God's chosen people, holy and dearly loved, clothe yourselves with compassion, kindness, humility, gentleness and patience. Bear with each other and forgive one another if any of you has a grievance against someone. Forgive as the Lord forgave you.

And over all these virtues put on love, which binds them all together in perfect unity. Let the peace of Christ rule in your hearts, since as members of one body you were called to peace. And be thankful."

Congratulations on completing the Transcend program. I pray that this workbook continues to be a resource for you moving forward. We are not promised that it will be easy in this life, and the enemy will work to place you back in the cycle of discontent. If you find yourself moving in that direction, revisit the materials and what you've accomplished through them. Most importantly, set another date with God and be real with Him.

This is our prayer for you as you continue from here:

✦ Romans 15:13: "May the God of hope fill you with all **joy** and **peace** as you trust in him, so that you may overflow with hope by the power of the Holy Spirit."

We welcome you to stay connected to us through social media and/or our website at www.istoriaministrygroup.org and share how God is moving in your story.

Thank you for being part of our story!

APPENDIX

My Story

Please record your answers to each assessment below.

Whole Health Assessment

Physical Health Score	Mental Health Score	Spiritual Health Score

Hurting Events

List your top five to ten hurting events from the "History of Hurting Events" section.

+ _____
+ _____
+ _____
+ _____
+ _____
+ _____
+ _____
+ _____
+ _____
+ _____

Results from Hurting Events

List your top three to five fears/lies from the "Fears/Lies List" section.

+ _____
+ _____
+ _____
+ _____
+ _____

List your top three to five feelings from hurts from the "Feelings List" section.

+ _____
+ _____
+ _____
+ _____
+ _____

List your top three to five reactions to hurts from the "Reactions List" section.

+ _____
+ _____
+ _____
+ _____
+ _____

List your top three to five needs resulting from hurts from the "Needs List" section.

+ _____
+ _____
+ _____
+ _____
+ _____

Assessment Results

Record your DISC assessment results below.

_____
_____
_____
_____
_____
_____

Record your Spiritual Gifts assessment results below.

_____
_____
_____
_____
_____
_____

Record your Love Languages assessment results below.

_____

_____

_____

_____

_____

_____

Answer Key

Chapter 1

surface-level; knower; God, people; peace

Chapter 2

joy; peace; 6000; perspective; truth; Bible; DNA; fine tuning; created; loves; plan; serve self; sin; separates; traps; solution; died; bridged; grace; believing; confessing; repenting; baptized; faithful

Chapter 3

spiritual; spirit; soul; body; renew; wounded feelings; threats to self; personalized injustices; anger; bitterness; repressing; suppressing; expressing; problem; renewing; transforming; forgive; fears; response; humility; empathy; self-acceptance; Renewal of Mind; Transforming of Heart; surrender; obedience

Chapter 4

Quiet time; pride, bitterness, unbelief

Chapter 5

God; people; convenience

I AM A CHILD
OF GOD

I AM FORGIVEN

I AM FREE F
ROM FEAR

I AM CONFIDENT
TO COME BEFORE
GOD IN PRAYER

I AM OBEDIENT
TO GOD

I AM CONFIDENT
IN THE BIBLE

I AM SURRENDERED

I AM SAVED

I AM GUIDED

I WILL PROTECT
MY HEART

If we confess our sins, he is faithful and just and will forgive us our sins and purify us from all unrighteousness.

– 1 John 1:9

Yet to all who did receive him, to those who believed in his name, he gave the right to become children of God

– John 1:12

If you remain in me and my words remain in you, ask whatever you wish, and it will be done for you.

– John 15:7

I sought the Lord, and he answered me; he delivered me from all my fears.

– Psalm 34:4

All Scripture is God-breathed and is useful for teaching, rebuking, correcting and training in righteousness.

– 2 Timothy 3:16

Whoever has my commands and keeps them is the one who loves me. The one who loves me will be loved by my Father, and I too will love them and show myself to them."

– John 14:21

For it is by grace you have been saved, through faith—and this is not from yourselves, it is the gift of God—not by works, so that no one can boast.

– Ephesians 2:8-9

I have been crucified with Christ and I no longer live, but Christ lives in me. The life I now live in the body, I live by faith in the Son of God, who loved me and gave himself for me.

– Galatians 2:20

Above all else, guard your heart, for everything you do flows from it.

– Proverbs 4:23

Trust in the Lord with all your heart and lean not on your own understanding; 6 in all your ways submit to him, and he will make your paths straight

– Proverbs 3:5-6

I AM SOUND
MINDED

I AM GUARDED
BY PEACE

I AM LIVING ON
PURPOSE

I AM ABLE

I AM LIVING FOR
AN AUDIENCE
OF ONE

I AM VICTORIOUS
OVER SIN

I AM LOVED

I AM HEARD

I AM NOT DEFINED
BY MY PAST

I WILL RENEW
MY MIND

Peace I leave with you; my peace I give you. I do not give to you as the world gives. Do not let your hearts be troubled and do not be afraid.

– John 14:27

For the Spirit God gave us does not make us timid, but gives us power, love and self-discipline

– 2 Timothy 1:7

I can do all this through him who gives me strength.

– Philippians 4:13

For we are God's handiwork, created in Christ Jesus to do good works, which God prepared in advance for us to do.

– Ephesians 2:10

No temptation has overtaken you except what is common to mankind. And God is faithful; he will not let you be tempted beyond what you can bear. But when you are tempted, he will also provide a way out so that you can endure it.

– 1 Corinthians 10:13

Am I now trying to win the approval of human beings, or of God? Or am I trying to please people? If I were still trying to please people, I would not be a servant of Christ.

– Galatians 1:10

This is the confidence we have in approaching God: that if we ask anything according to his will, he hears us.

– 1 John 5:14

But God demonstrates his own love for us in this: While we were still sinners, Christ died for us.

– Romans 5:8

Do not conform to the pattern of this world, but be transformed by the renewing of your mind. Then you will be able to test and approve what God's will is—His good, pleasing and perfect will.

– Romans 12:2

Therefore, if anyone is in Christ, the new creation has come: The old has gone, the new is here!

– 2 Corinthians 5:17

The first evidence for the existence of God is something that David mentioned three thousand years ago in Psalm 19:

"The heavens proclaim the glory of God. The skies display his craftsmanship. Day after day they continue to speak; night after night they make him known. They speak without a sound or word; their voice is never heard. Yet their message has gone throughout the earth, and their words to all the world" (Psalm 19:1-4, New Living Translation).

David says that the heavens (the stars) testify to the fact that there is a Creator.

Abraham Lincoln said, "I can see how it might be possible for a man to look down upon Earth and be an atheist, but I cannot conceive how he could look up into the heavens and say that there is no God."

As Christians, we believe that God has made Himself known through both natural and special revelation. Natural revelation is God revealed in nature. Arguments from nature include:

+ the cosmological argument,

+ the fine-tuning argument,

+ and the moral argument—not only does God exist, but life was created with a purpose, not by accident.

God has made Himself known even clearer through special revelation. Natural theology provides a compelling case for God's existence, but Judaism and Islam also use these arguments. That's why we need special revelation to answer the question "Who is God?" more precisely.

Let's look at four indisputable features of the world to see this convincing evidence.

1.   **The universe had a beginning.**

     Through the centuries, philosophers and scientists have concluded that there are really only three different possibilities to explain the universe's existence:

     ☞ It has always existed. No need for God. The universe has always been around.

     ☞ It created itself. Again, no need for God. It brought itself into existence.

     ☞ It was created by a spiritual creative agent, God.

     Let's walk through all of these options and consider which one is the most reasonable.

2.   **The universe has always existed or is eternal.**

     This theory has been rejected by the scientific community. It's not pastors who scratched this option off. The scientific community did! Why? Well, one thing both atheistic and theistic scientists agree on is that everything which has a beginning has a cause, meaning that something else intervened to bring it into existence. Therefore, anything that has existed forever needs no cause. There was no start to it; therefore, nothing caused it to exist.

3.   **The universe created itself.**

     In this theory, the universe needs no cause—no need for an intelligent designer and no need for an explanation. It simply created itself.

With this theory, God needs no cause. So, a Christian would ask an atheist, "Where did the universe come from?"

The atheist would respond, "It's always been there; it doesn't need to come from anywhere. Where did God come from?"

The Christian would say, "He's always been there; He doesn't need to come from anywhere."

Christians and atheists both agree that everything which has a beginning has a cause, and anything that has existed forever needs no cause.

Atheist scientists are repulsed and laugh at the thought that Christians do not believe that the universe existed forever. However, an astronomer named Edwin Hubble discovered something fascinating—some stars were redder than they should be. As scientists studied this phenomenon more, they realized that these stars were traveling at incredible speeds away from us, resulting in their color.

This is called the Doppler Effect. When a car is moving towards you, the sound is higher-pitched, and as the car moves away from you, it is lower-pitched. This is because the sound waves are compressed moving towards you and spread out moving away from you.

Hubble determined that the odd color was because of the Doppler Effect, and the stars were moving away at a rapid pace.

How was this possible? He then concluded that the universe was expanding.

Well, if the universe is currently expanding, that means it used to be smaller. If you take it back many years, this means it had to have started from a single point. This was so unexpected and unwelcome that many preeminent scientists mocked it, including Fred Hoyle, one of the great astronomers at the time, who—according to colleagues Ralph Alpher and Robert Herman—jokingly called the theory the "Big Bang theory." During this time period, the Big Bang theory was developed. The universe started from a single point, exploded, and rapidly expanded.

Scientists hated to hear this but slowly came to accept that the universe is expanding, and thus, it had a beginning. If it had a beginning, what does that mean? Something had to initiate the start of it.

Fred Hoyle was an atheist until Hubble's discovery.

Stephen Hawking, the renowned late astronomer from Cambridge University, agreed that this is the consensus. He said, "Almost everyone believes that the universe, and time itself, had a beginning."

Astrophysicist Robert Jastrow, a self-described agnostic, stated, "The seed of everything that has happened in the Universe was planted in that first instant; every star, every planet and every living creature in the Universe came into being as a result of events that were set in motion in the moment of the cosmic explosion... The Universe flashed into being, and we cannot find out what caused that to happen."

Now, the understanding that the universe is expanding is accepted among most scientists.

This is in perfect harmony with what the Bible says in the very first verse: "In the beginning, God created the heavens and the earth" (Genesis 1:1).

So, now we must ask: what caused it to begin?

Scientists have no explanation for the sudden explosion of light and matter. Then, we look to the second option: that the universe created itself.

Richard Dawkins states that "the universe evolved literally out of nothing."

Nothing! Stephen Hawking repeated this sentiment, saying that the universe came from "nothing."

These men, considered by some to be two of the brightest atheists of our time, claimed, "Once there was nothing, and that nothingness turned itself into all the billions of galaxies, stars, and planets making up the entire universe."

This is just pure foolishness! Options A and B can be thrown out purely on scientific and philosophical grounds. And so we conclude (almost by default) that option C (God created the universe) is the most reasonable option.

4. **God had no beginning and existed forever.**

If nothing cannot produce something and yet something exists (e.g. the universe), then a creative agent must have *always* existed in order to bring that which exists into being. Think of it this way:

☝ If there ever was a time when absolutely nothing existed, nothing would exist now.

☝ Something exists now.

☝ Therefore, there was never a time that absolutely nothing existed.

We have no problem believing that God is the One who always existed. Because this is the case, the answer to the question "Who made God?" is no one. God is eternal and does not need a maker. The universe, though, is *not* eternal and therefore does require a maker.

Scientists have no explanation for the sudden explosion of light and matter. The Bible tells us that God created matter, space, and time. As science progresses, I believe it will agree with the Bible more and more, and find that the truth aligns with its teachings.

✦ Genesis 1:1: "In the beginning God created the heavens and the earth."

☝ A Hebrew word for create or make is "bara," meaning "creation from nothing."

- Another Hebrew word for create or make is "asah," meaning to fashion or make something suitable.

✦ Genesis 1:2: "Now the earth was formless and empty, darkness was over the surface of the deep, and the Spirit of God was hovering over the waters."

✦ Gen 1:3: "And God said, 'Let there be light,' and there was light."

This leads us to our second feature of the world we'll look at, the conditions for life.

The Conditions For Life—The Fine-Tuning of the Cosmos

Romans 1:19-20: "... since what may be known about God is plain to them, because God has made it plain to them. For since the creation of the world God's invisible qualities—his eternal power and divine nature—have been clearly seen, being understood from what has been made, so that people are without excuse."

This is called the cosmological argument. The more science discovers, the more scientists are impressed by the fact that the universe has been designed for the specific benefit of life—human beings in particular (also referred to as the Anthropic Principle).

Many renowned scientists are able to acknowledge this argument:

Stephen Hawking, physicist: "The initial state of the Universe must have been very carefully chosen indeed if the hot big bang model was correct right back to the beginning of time. It would be very difficult to explain why the Universe should have begun in just this way, except as the act of a God who intended to create beings like us."

Freeman Dyson, world-renowned scientist: "The more I examine the Universe and study the details of its architecture, the more evidence I find that the Universe in some sense must have known we were coming."

Paul Davies, physicist, cosmologist, and astrobiologist: "It seems as though somebody has fine-tuned nature's numbers to make the Universe... The impression of design is overwhelming."

Many constants of our planet are so precise that if they were even slightly different, human life could not exist. In that certainty, the cosmological argument strengthens.

1. "Cosmological" comes from the term "cosmos," which means the universe.

2. The term also comes from the root of the word "cosmetic."

   - "Cosmetic" means skilled in ordering or arranging.

   - Somewhat related is cosmetology, the study and application of beauty treatment. Its meaning is to be ordered and beautiful, as is the foundation of that industry.

The universe is more elegant and more finely-tuned than we could have ever imagined. The probability of having a life-sustaining planet is virtually infinitesimal, and many scientists are starting to see that the only way this could have happened was as a result of some kind of creator who could form these complex pieces into a place capable of supporting human life. There's enough evidence that even non-Christians can't ignore the truth. One such man, Stephen Hawking, said, "The universe and the laws of physics seem to have been specifically designed for us. If any of about forty physical qualities had more than slightly different values, life as we know it could not exist: Either atoms would not be stable, or they wouldn't combine into molecules, or the stars wouldn't form the heavier elements, or the universe would collapse before life could develop, and so on."

When Hawking speaks of the "forty physical qualities" that appear to have been specifically designed to permit life, he's referring to:

+ *The force of gravity*—If it was much stronger, then everything would collapse. If it was much weaker, everything would drift apart.

+ *The speed of light and the mass of an electron*—If the speed of light or the mass of an electron were even slightly different, there would be no planet capable of supporting human life.

+ *The force that binds subatomic particles (such as neutrons and protons) together within the nuclei of atoms*—If the force were stronger or weaker by more than about one percent, the universe would be either all hydrogen or have no hydrogen at all.

+ *The energy levels in carbon atoms*—They're just right for life to exist; change them a little, and the universe would be incapable of supporting life.

When it comes to these kinds of conditions, Dr. Francis Collins, the former head of the Human Genome Project, states that if any of these constants "was off by even one part in a million, or in some cases, by one part in a million million... there would have been no galaxy, stars, planets or people."

Why is the universe so orderly and so reliable?

+ Isaiah 45:18: "For this is what the Lord says—he who created the heavens, he is God; he who fashioned and made the earth, he founded it; he did not create it to be empty, but formed it to be inhabited—he says: 'I am the Lord, and there is no other...'"

✦ Psalm 115:16: "The highest heavens belong to the Lord, but the earth he has given to mankind."

The more scientists study the universe, the more they discover that conditions in the universe appear to have been extremely fine-tuned to permit life. Even the greatest scientists have been struck by how strange this is. Richard Feynman, a Nobel Prize winner for quantum electrodynamics, said, "Why nature is mathematical is a mystery... The fact that there are rules at all is a kind of miracle." There is no logical necessity for a universe that obeys rules, let alone one that abides by the rules of mathematics.

Isaiah 45:12: "It is I who made the earth and created mankind on it. My own hands stretched out the heavens; I marshaled their starry hosts."

Scientists have identified numerous conditions that require just the right values—in other words, they need to be "tuned" to just the right degree—for any kind of conceivable physical life to exist in the universe. If any of these conditions were to change even a little, the universe would be hostile to life and incapable of supporting it. This conclusion is not something Christian scientists concocted; this is being acknowledged by scientists of every persuasion.

"Well, maybe the universe just ended up this way by chance! You know, after it sprang into existence from nothing, by accident."

And perhaps not. Donald Page of Princeton's Institute for Advanced Science calculated the odds against our universe randomly taking a form suitable for life as one in ten billion to the 124th power!

These are such astronomical odds that it's safe to say the universe did *not* end up with these finely-tuned conditions without having an incredibly intelligent and powerful designer. That's what many cosmologists and physicists are concluding today: something supernatural appears to be going on behind the scenes.

Well, this conclusion that God may be behind it all, of course, does not sit well with atheists, so how do they explain the fine-tuning of the universe? They acknowledge that what appears to be "fine-tuning" exists. Richard Dawkins, Stephen Hawking, and other prominent atheists came up with a hypothesis straight out of science fiction called "the multiverse."

What's the multiverse hypothesis? Their "multiverse" hypothesis says there might be trillions of universes (thus "many-verses") and that somewhere in this gigantic mix of universes, a finely-tuned universe appears by chance. We humans just *happen* to live in that finely-tuned universe. What evidence is there for a multiverse, meaning universes outside our own? There is *no evidence to support this*. There is not a shred of evidence for even one universe outside our own, let alone trillions of universes. They tout their interest in observational evidence, but when faced with the observational evidence of the universe's fine-tuning, they have no observational evidence to support it. They have no answer for how *those* universes came into existence.

The multiverse theory does nothing to undermine or weaken the case that the incredible fine-tuning of the universe is indeed compelling evidence for the existence of God.

The Third Piece of Proof of the Existence of God—
An Information-Rich Sphere Where We Live

Let's consider the facts about cells and the DNA code that informs and programs a cell's behavior:

1. All living things are made up of cells.

2. Each cell contains DNA.

    *   DNA is a three-billion-lettered program telling the cell to act in a certain way. It is a full instruction manual.

- DNA is made up of four chemicals that are arranged a certain way in human cells.

- There are three billion of these letters in every human cell.

3. DNA instructs the cell.

- DNA does this similarly to how you can program your phone to beep for specific reasons.

In every cell of our bodies there exists a very detailed instruction code, much like a miniature computer program. A computer program is made up of ones and zeros (the binary code), and the way the code is arranged tells the computer program what to do. One has to ask: how did this information program wind up in each human cell? These are not just chemicals. These are chemicals that instruct! They code in a very detailed way exactly how the person's body should develop.

A. Evolutionists say everything, in all of its complexity, was created by chance.

As biologist Jacques Monod, a Nobel prize winner, puts it, "Chance *alone* is at the source of every innovation, of all creation in the biosphere. Pure chance, absolutely free but blind, (no purpose and design) [is] at the very root of the stupendous edifice of evolution."

Chance means there is no design or designer. Since Darwin's early work, *On the Origin of Species*, evolution has been linked with random processes. Think of how absurd that is.

That's like saying a tornado went through a junkyard and out popped a 747 Airplane. That *Messiah* composed itself apart from Handel. That *The Last Supper* painted itself, without Leonardo da Vinci. Science is revealing more and more that the theory of accidental causation is flawed. The idea of forming a simple protein, let alone the DNA, let alone the cell, and on top of that, highly-functioning human beings by chance is utterly impossible. You cannot find instruction or precise information like this without someone intentionally constructing it. If they reject "chance," then what do they put in its place?

Richard Dawkins, a critic of creationism, believes in something called the "blind forces of physics." This essentially means that life spontaneously arose from nonlife. It proposes gradual and random transformations that occur from simple beginnings to complex ones. That would mean that humans and other living species are descended from bacteria... and that over long periods of time, different kinds of animals and plants have supposedly developed as a result of small changes, resulting in an *increase* in genetic information all of the way from bacteria to where we are today.

B. This process is called natural selection and mutations.

Natural selection

This process is where only the strongest organisms tend to survive and produce more offspring, thereby earning the nickname, "survival of the fittest." This theory first came from Charles Darwin and is now believed to be the main process that brings about evolution.

Mutations

A mutation is a change in DNA, thereby influencing our instruction manual. For a plant to evolve into a person, it has to have increased in the amount of DNA information. Evolutionists say mutations somehow provide this new information. By that logic, mutations are essential to evolution.

However, mutations do not add information! In fact, scientists such as Dr. Lee Spetner and Dr. Werner Gitt admitted that in all of their research and studies, they've never found a mutation that *added* information. Instead, it reduced information. What does this mean? Without the intelligent input to increase information, natural selection would not work as a mechanism for evolution—it would produce a totally different kind of being since we know that information cannot arise from non-information.

Macroevolution

Evolutionists believe that one species can turn into a totally different species with DNA that did not exist before. Yet, this has *never* been observed. A cat has never been seen turning into a dog.

Microevolution

The Bible actually does teach this, acknowledging that there can be changes *within* a species. An example would be the varieties of dogs that came about from an original dog. This is observable and biblical. The Bible says that they "produced after their own kind." Take a look at Gen 1:24: "And God said, 'Let the land produce living creatures according to their kinds: the livestock, the creatures that move along the ground, and the wild animals, each according to its kind.' And it was so." This only operates on the information that the creatures already contained that gene, thereby not producing new information.

Evolutionists will say, "Well, over time, the information will form." However, scientist Dr. Werner Gitt admits that it *always* takes greater information to produce information, and ultimately, information is the result of intelligence: "There is no known law of nature, no known process and no known sequence of events which can cause information to originate by itself into matter."

The universe had a beginning; it's clear in the pages of the Bible:

✦ Psalms 90:2: "Before the mountains were born or you brought forth the whole world, from everlasting to everlasting you are God."

✦ Psalms 33:6: "By the word of the Lord the heavens were made, their starry host by the breath of his mouth."

✦ Psalms 33:8: "Let all the earth fear the Lord; let all the people of the world revere him."

✦ Psalms 33:9: "For he spoke, and it came to be; he commanded, and it stood firm."

With the fine-tuning of the cosmos, many scientists are starting to see that the only way this could have happened was as a result of some kind of fine-tuner and creator.

God Does Not Force Us to Believe in Him

Instead, God has provided sufficient proof of His existence for us to willingly respond to Him: the information-rich sphere in which we live, aka our planet. Life requires a minimum level of complexity, structure, and design. The idea of forming a simple protein by chance, let alone an entire human race, animals, and plants, is utterly impossible. You cannot find instruction or precise information like this without someone intentionally constructing it.

Reliability of the Bible

The Bible is notably an *incredible book*. It is the best-selling, most quoted, most published, most circulated, most translated, and most influential book in the history of mankind. There is no close second.

If God exists and put us here on Earth, wouldn't we assume He would want to reveal Himself to us and instruct us on how to live this life He's provided? If they are the very words from God, they would be the ultimate source of truth. Would He not supernaturally preserve His word throughout all generations? Think about it.

Are *you* able to preserve important financial papers (e.g. taxes, property records, etc.)? The National Archives is able to protect important documents and artifacts from America's history. Do you have your birth certificate? You need it for a driver's license or passport. This all seems obvious to consider, but if God can create the universe—and all life within it—surely He can preserve His Word for all generations!

Jesus promised:

+ Matthew 24:35: "Heaven and earth will pass away, but my words will never pass away."

+ 1 Peter 1:24-25: "'All people are like grass, and all their glory is like the flowers of the field; the grass withers and the flowers fall, but the word of the Lord endures forever.' And this is the word that was preached to you."

The evidence is clear in their words, but how can we *know* that the Bible isn't just an ancient book of fiction? How can we know that it hasn't been changed throughout the centuries? And what makes it different from the Quran or the Book of Mormon?

We will look at evidence that demonstrates, in its totality, that the Bible is indeed what it claims to be: the trustworthy Word of God—written by men, yes—but men who were guided by God as they penned its words.

- ✦ 2 Peter 1:21: "For prophecy never had its origin in the human will, but prophets, though human, spoke from God as they were carried along by the Holy Spirit."

- ✦ 2 Timothy 3:16: "All Scripture is God-breathed and is useful for teaching, rebuking, correcting and training in righteousness..."

The Old Testament

At the time of Christ, Jewish people already accepted the Old Testament as divinely inspired and complete.

How was the Old Testament formed and preserved?

It began with the books of Moses. After Moses wrote the books, he commanded that the books of the law be placed in the Ark of the Covenant for preservation (Deuteronomy 31:24-26). As the remaining books were written, they too were kept by the Ark! The Old Testament books we have today existed from that time and into the time of our Lord and the apostles.

Jesus verified its authority and completion:

- ✦ Luke 24:27: "And beginning with Moses and all the Prophets, he explained to them what was said in all the Scriptures concerning himself."

- ✦ Luke 24:44: "He said to them, 'This is what I told you while I was still with you: Everything must be fulfilled that is written about me in the Law of Moses, the Prophets and the Psalms.'"

Not only Jesus, but Jewish historians such as Josephus from the 1st century and ancient commentaries confirmed that the 22 books of the Old Testament were divinely inspired and are the same books since in the days of Ezra. Since no other prophet came after Malachi, no other words from God were given—until Christ.

It's clear in the New Testament. Hebrews 1:1-2 states, "In the past God spoke to our ancestors through the prophets at many times and in various ways, but in these last days he has spoken to us by his Son, whom he appointed heir of all things, and through whom also he made the universe."

Matthew 17:4-5 says, "Listen to him!" That's because Jesus is the *last* prophet God spoke through, which is why any teaching contrary to what Jesus taught is *false*.

✦ Galatians 1:8-9: "But even if we or an angel from heaven should preach a gospel other than the one we preached to you, let them be under God's curse!"

Here is the criteria used to determine which writings were indeed inspired by God and to be recognized as scripture:

✦ **Eyewitnesses:**

☞ Only those who had witnessed the events or had recorded eyewitness testimony could have their writings considered as Holy Scripture.

✦ **Acceptance:** Was the book widely accepted and used by the churches?

☞ Any book that claimed to be God's word—yet diverted from the truth of the life of Christ—would have been rejected by Jesus' own disciples.

- ✦ **Consistency**: Did the book contain consistency of doctrine and teaching to that of Christ and His apostles or did it contradict it?
  - ☞ If it wasn't in agreement, it was eliminated.

Since Jesus taught that God preserved the Old Testament for His people, we can also be assured that God took the same care in preserving the New Testament books. When the evidence is examined, we find it consistent and credible.

Manuscripts

We don't have the original manuscript. This is not unusual though, as other historical documents don't have the originals either. Over the years, the original manuscripts have been lost or destroyed with age. Therefore, the question is: how accurate are the copies that we have?

1. **The accuracy of the Bible based on the number of manuscripts**

    Why is the number of manuscripts important? The more manuscripts we find, the more we can see that the manuscripts match perfectly with other manuscripts found in other countries throughout Europe, Asia, and Africa.

    First, let's compare it to a few other historical manuscripts:

    Julius Caesar wrote a historical account about his military campaigns against the Gallic tribes. *The Gallic Wars* was written in about 44 BC. We never found the original manuscript he wrote, but we found some copies. The earliest copy found was from 900 AD, 940 years after the original was written. We've only found 10 other copies, yet nobody doubts the accuracy or the authenticity of *The Gallic Wars*!

Plato wrote a historical account in 347 BC. We never found the original, but we did find fragments of some of the copies. The earliest copy we have is from 900 AD, 1200 years after the original was written. Only 20 copies or fragments were found.

Aristotle wrote some historical documents in 322 BC. We have only found 49 copies, but again, nobody doubts the historical accounts of Plato and Aristotle.

Now let's talk about the Bible.

How many copies, or fragments of copies, of just the New Testament have we found over the years? *24,000.* That's thousands of copies and fragments!

You can see these in museums around the world, with the exception of a few that are likely kept in the Vatican. Of those 24,000 copies and fragments, 5,000 of them are in the original Greek and the rest in other languages. The manuscript evidence for the Bible positively dwarfs the manuscript evidence for all other books of antiquity!

The Bible has more manuscript evidence to support it than any 10 pieces of classical literature combined. As the years go by, we find more and more fragments and copies, and as we find more, we are able to further verify our translations.

2. **The accuracy of the Bible based on the consistent content in the manuscripts**

How do we know that these copies and fragments are all copied correctly? Well, when we took the copies we found and compared them to each other, we found that we have less than 1% of a difference. There were only some spelling errors or repeated words. The copy found in Europe has a 99% match with a copy found in Africa, which has a 99% match to a copy found in Asia. This tells us that the Bible we have today is within 1% accuracy of the original version. It also throws out all of the theories of those who say that the Bible was rewritten to say whatever the writers wanted it to say.

If that was true, these writers would have had to travel to all of those places around the world, find every copy of the Bible they didn't like, burn them, and replace them with their new, edited version. It seems a little far-fetched, right?

Examples of Consistency: This is a huge discovery.

The Dead Sea Scrolls contain the oldest known copies of the Old Testament. Over 200 clay pots were found containing handwritten manuscripts, dating back to 200 BC. Almost the entire Old Testament was found. The best evidence prior to this was from the 8th century AD. They now discovered manuscripts 1,000 years earlier than what they currently had thought. When they compared the text to the one they had from the 8th century AD to that of 200 BC, they discovered the accuracy in their copies of their translations was 99.999% pure.

In the last 50 years, we have discovered through archeology over 3,500 complete manuscripts of the New Testament across three continents. Compared to the copies we have today, it is 99% accurate and the only changed content had no theological significance, i.e. limited to punctuation changes here or there. There is no other religion in the world that can match this accuracy of manuscripts.

If you look at Buddhism as an example, as it moved from India where it originated to China, Vietnam and so on, it absorbed much of the local religions. Therefore, it mutated and changed over time to adapt to the different cultures that it was being taken to. Over time, the religion has evolved and changed.

People sometimes say that "Christianity needs to evolve to stay with the times." To that, I ask, "How can it?" First of all, Christianity is based on the manuscript. The manuscript itself is not mutating or changing. Second, the morals don't change. If it was immoral for me to kill 8,000 years ago, it's still immoral for me to kill today. Third, God has not changed! "Jesus Christ is the same yesterday and today and forever" (Hebrews 13:8).

There are countless facts to verify that the Bible we have today is accurate and reflects what the original author wrote:

✦ **Fact:** The Bible has been translated into various other languages.

  ☞ We have more than 15,000 existing copies of the various translations written in the Latin and Syriac (Christian Aramaic), some of which were written as early as 150 A.D. There are coptic translations from as early as the 3rd and 4th centuries, Armenian translations from 400 A.D., from the Gothic 4th century, the Georgian 5th century, the Ethiopic 6th century, and the Nubian 6th century.

  ☞ With this many translations, it would have been almost impossible to corrupt or forge its contents without it being largely noticeable. They would have to gather all of the translations from all areas and change each one. What we find is the Gospel didn't significantly change even in the translation to other languages!

✦ **Fact:** The Bible is the most-quoted document in the entire history of man.

  ☞ When a pastor, priest, or someone else writes a sermon, they often will quote the Bible, and the early church fathers did this as well. We have found, in total, 86,489 quotes from the early church fathers.

🖑 If you went through all of the old documents of the church leaders and the sermons prior to the 3rd Century and started reassembling the Bible from the mentions in them, you'd be able to reconstruct all but 11 verses of the entire New Testament.

And here's what is most important: *all of those match the manuscripts we have today!*

3. **The accuracy of the Bible based on how manuscripts were created**

The ancient Jewish people have preserved the Old Testament as no other manuscript has ever been preserved. Although it was first written on perishable materials, it had to be copied and recopied for hundreds of years before the invention of the printing press. There were special men—scribes, lawyers, massoretes—whose sole duty it was to preserve and transmit these documents with practically perfect fidelity. The manuscripts were meticulously copied, counting the letters, syllables, and words. So much so, that if they made one error in copying a sentence, they destroyed the whole page. The Scriptures have never diminished in style or correctness after hundreds and hundreds of years!

Compare it to Shakespeare's 37 plays; there's dispute over the hundreds of readings that affect their meaning.

As Christians, we can be confident. If God wanted us to have His word, He would supernaturally make sure it was preserved.

Preserved Through Persecution

Many have tried to burn the Bible, ban it, and outlaw it from the days of Romans to present-day Communistic countries. French infidel, Voltaire, who died in 1778, declared that 100 years in the future, Christianity would be swept from existence and passed into history. Fifty years after his death, the Geneva Bible Society used Voltaire's press and house to produce stacks of Bibles. "Heaven and earth will pass away, but my words will never pass away" (Mark 13:31).

In summation, the Bible we have today can be trusted to be what God originally inspired its authors to write. Based on manuscript evidence, we see the accuracy of the Bible because of the number of manuscripts, the consistency of its content across the globe, and because of how the manuscripts were written.

Based on manuscript evidence, a Christian can take the whole Bible in their hand and say, without fear or hesitation, that they hold in it the true Word of God, handed down without essential loss from generation to generation throughout the centuries.

The Reliability of the Bible: Prophecy and Statistics

The 3ʳᵈ and 4ᵗʰ principles of our MAPS (Manuscripts, Archaeology, Prophecy, Statistics) acronym in Bible reliability are those of prophecy and statistics.

We've seen strong scientific evidence that God exists based on the four indisputable features of the world. If God exists, then He would want to reveal Himself to us and give us truth concerning the four basic questions of life. If God chose to reveal this truth to us, then He would supernaturally preserve His word throughout all generations, which we've seen in both the manuscript and archeological evidence.

We believe the Bible is that truth—God's Word! But for centuries, people have tried to disprove the Bible, claiming that the Bible is simply a book written by men, just as any other book.

So, what makes the Bible unique from any other writing? Don't other books claim to be words from a god/god(s)?

+ Mormons: The Book of Mormon

+ Unification church followers: Divine Principle by Sun Myung Moon

+ Muslims: Quran

+ Scientologists: Dianetics: The Modern Science of Mental Health

+ Hindus: The Vedas

+ Jehovah's Witnesses: The Watchtower

What proves the Bible differs from all these other writings and is God's word?

Prophecy! Prophecy is a prediction of the future from special knowledge that comes from God.

God said the criteria to distinguish His truth from false prophets who also claim to have truth from a god is fulfilled prophecy!

God gives a test to determine if a truth *is from God or not*. It's found in:

+ Deuteronomy 18:9-22: "The Lord said to me: 'What they say is good. I will raise up for them a prophet like you from among their fellow Israelites, and I will put my words in his mouth.'"

+ Hebrews 1:1-2: "In the past God spoke to our ancestors through the prophets at many times and in various ways, but in these last days he has spoken to us by his Son, whom he appointed heir of all things, and through whom also he made the universe."

The people asked, "How will we know whether he is a true prophet or not?" God said that if a prophet makes a prediction and it does not happen, he is a false prophet: "If what a prophet proclaims in the name of the Lord does not take place or come true, that is a message the Lord has not spoken. That prophet has spoken presumptuously, so do not be alarmed" (Deuteronomy 18:22).

Because only God knows the future.

It's stated in Isaiah 46:9-10: "Remember the former things, those of long ago; I am God, and there is no other; I am God, and there is none like me. I make known the end from the beginning, from ancient times, what is still to come..."

And then again in Isaiah 41:22-24: "Tell us, you idols, what is going to happen. Tell us what the former things were, so that we may consider them and know their final outcome. Or declare to us the things to come, tell us what the future holds, so we may know that you are gods. Do something, whether good or bad, so that we will be dismayed and filled with fear. But you are less than nothing and your works are utterly worthless; whoever chooses you is detestable."

Isaiah 45:21-22: "Declare what is to be, present it—let them take counsel together. Who foretold this long ago, who declared it from the distant past? Was it not I, the Lord? And there is no God apart from me, a righteous God and a Savior; there is none but me. 'Turn to me and be saved, all you ends of the earth; for I am God, and there is no other...'"

Wouldn't it make sense that God would give a test to distinguish between His words and anyone else who claims to be a god? Since only God is all-knowing, it would make sense that the test would be to tell what would happen in the years to come in specific detail, apart from man causing it. So when someone claims to be a prophet of God and that God gave them the truth, this list will determine if (s)he is a true or false prophet.

Be wary if they make:

- ✦ **Declarations of what God will do** to people after they die or after the end of world history because though it's predictive prophecy, we cannot verify it from historical facts right now.

- ✦ **Vague predictions of events** in which people or places are not specifically named because this is not clearly verifiable.

- ✦ **Declarations of what humans plan to do themselves** because this is not predictive prophecy from God but is merely human plans that are then self-fulfilled (i.e. someone claiming that next year, they will go to Mecca to worship).

Therefore, the fulfilled predictive prophecy must:

- ✦ Be specific so it can be historically verified.

- ✦ It *must* be accurately fulfilled because if it is not, then it is clearly not a prophecy from God.

  - ☝ When you put the Bible to this test, you will see that the Bible is unique in its fulfilled prophecy.

God supernaturally put His imprint on Scripture by prophesying events hundreds and hundreds of years *before* they took place, which we have since seen and verified in history. In fact, some critics ask, "Couldn't someone just have written these down and pretend they were written earlier?" However, manuscripts have been found that confirm that these various prophecies were written down 400-1,000 years before they actually occurred. This includes the many predictions of Christ's birth, life, and death, which were indisputably written down more than a century before they occurred.

The discovery of the Dead Sea Scrolls proves the predictions with the book of Isaiah. Some people ask, "Were these originally intended to be Messianic prophecies?" Since some of the prophecies occur as part of the text of a story, it's a natural question, as well as the following: "How do you know these are Messianic prophecies? Couldn't someone have read these texts after Jesus came along and *claimed* they are Messianic prophecies?"

The reason we know these texts were intended to be Messianic prophecies is because they were recognized (and discussed) by Jews before Jesus' birth. These were verses Jews themselves recognized as Messianic verses. So it's clearly not something written down after Jesus was born, died, and resurrected!

Of all the attacks that have ever been made upon the Scripture, there has never been one book written by a skeptic that disproves the prophecies of the Bible.

Hundreds of prophecies, some given hundreds of years in advance, have been fulfilled to date. Numerous Old Testament prophecies have been fulfilled, including the destruction of Edom (Obadiah 1), the curse on Babylon (Isaiah 13), the destruction of Tyre (Ezekiel 26) and Nineveh (Hah. 103). The time and nature of Christ's birth was foretold in the Old Testament, as were dozens of other things about His life, death, and resurrection in Daniel 9, Micah 5:2, and Isaiah 53. Jesus predicted his own death, burial, and resurrection!

This fulfilled prophecy is the most powerful evidence of the unique divine authority of the Bible. In no other religious writings in the world do we find any specific predictive prophecies like we find in the Bible. This proves that the Bible is uniquely superior to any and all other books.

Old Testament Prophecies

An Old Testament scholar, J. Barton Payne, identifies 737 separate prophecies in the Bible. Of these, he claims that there are 594 Bible prophecies fulfilled already. That's more than 80%.

Tyre was a Phoenician city on the Mediterranean Sea that had great hatred for the people of Israel. It was the subject of many prophecies that came to pass.

A. Tyre's fortresses would fail.

In Amos 1:9-10, the Lord says, "For three sins of Tyre, even for four, I will not relent. Because she sold whole communities of captives to Edom, disregarding a treaty of brotherhood, I will send fire on the walls of Tyre that will consume her fortresses." The prophet was saying that God would cause Tyre's protective fortresses to fail as punishment for the way that Tyre treated Israel.

The prophecy was written in about 750 BC. The prophecy was then fulfilled in 586-573 BC when Babylonian King Nebuchadnezzar attacked the mainland of Tyre and in 333-332 BC when Alexander the Great conquered the island of Tyre. Alexander's army built a land bridge from the mainland to the island so that they could use a battering ram to break through the island's fortress.

B. Tyre would be attacked by many nations.

This prophecy is clear in Ezekiel 26:3: "... therefore this is what the Sovereign Lord says: I am against you, Tyre, and I will bring many nations against you, like the sea casting up its waves."

The prophecy was written between 587 and 586 BC, and it was later fulfilled many times over. At about the time that Ezekiel delivered this prophecy, Babylon had begun a 13-year attack on Tyre's mainland. Later, in about 332 BC, Alexander the Great conquered the island of Tyre and brought an end to the Phoenician Empire.

C. Tyre's stones, timber, and soil would be cast into the sea.

Ezekiel 26:12 demonstrates this: "They will plunder your wealth and loot your merchandise; they will break down your walls and demolish your fine houses and throw your stones, timber and rubble into the sea."

The prophecy was written between 587 and 586 BC, and it was later fulfilled in 333-332 BC. Ezekiel's prophecy accurately describes how Alexander the Great built a land bridge from the mainland to the island of Tyre, when he attacked in 333-332 BC. Then the next prophecy described how Alexander's forces would take rubble (stones, timber, soil) from Tyre's mainland and toss it into the sea to build the land bridge (which is still there) and continue their siege.

D. Tyre would lose its power over the sea.

Zechariah 9:3-4 states, "Tyre has built herself a stronghold; she has heaped up silver like dust, and gold like the dirt of the streets. But the Lord will take away her possessions and destroy her power on the sea, and she will be consumed by fire."

The prophecy was written between 520 and 518 BC, and it was fulfilled following 332 BC. The prophet said that the Phoenician city of Tyre would lose its status as a powerful nation on the Mediterranean Sea. Today, there is still a city called Tyre that is either on, or near, the original Phoenician site, but this Tyre is a small city in modern-day Lebanon. It is certainly not the powerful nation that it was in the days of Zechariah.

E. Phoenician Tyre would never again be found.

We know this to be true from Ezekiel 26:21: "I will bring you to a horrible end and you will be no more. You will be sought, but you will never again be found, declares the Sovereign Lord."

The prophecy was written between 587-586 BC, and it was fulfilled after 332 BC. The prophet knew that the Phoenician city of Tyre would be brought to an end and would never again be found. When Alexander the Great destroyed the city in 332 BC, he brought an end to the Phoenician Empire. The empire was never revived or "found" again.

As for the city itself, it has been torn down and built upon by a succession of foreign powers. Today, finding artifacts from the original Phoenician Tyre is difficult. According to the *Columbia Encyclopedia, Fifth Edition*: "The principal ruins of the city today are those of buildings erected by the Crusaders. There are some Greco-Roman remains, but any left by the Phoenicians lie underneath the present town."

F. Phoenician Tyre would never be rebuilt.

The prophecy makes it clear in Ezekiel 26:14: "I will make you a bare rock, and you will become a place to spread fishnets. You will never be rebuilt, for I the Lord have spoken, declares the Sovereign Lord."

The prophecy was written between 587-586 BC, and it has been fulfilled since 332 BC. The prophet says the Phoenician city of Tyre would be destroyed and never be rebuilt. This was fulfilled when Alexander the Great conquered Tyre in 332 BC and the Phoencian Empire was never able to recover from the attack.

Tyre recovered in a measure from this blow but never regained the place it had previously held in the world. The larger part of the site of the once-great city is now bare as the top of a rock. Other nations and empires have built and rebuilt cities on or near the original Phoenician site.

John C. Beck keeps the history of the island city of Tyre in the proper perspective: "The history of Tyre does not stop after the conquest of Alexander. Men continue to rebuild her and armies continue to besiege her walls until finally, after 1,600 years, she falls never to be rebuilt again."

2. The Destruction of Babylon

When Isaiah predicted the destruction of Babylon in the 8th century BC, it was over a hundred years away from becoming a world power. Today, it is just a small province in what is modern-day southern Iraq.

A. Babylon would rule Judah for 70 years.

It's written in the Bible passage Jeremiah 25:11-12: "This whole country will become a desolate wasteland, and these nations will serve the king of Babylon seventy years. 'But when the seventy years are fulfilled, I will punish the king of Babylon and his nation, the land of the Babylonians, for their guilt,' declares the Lord, 'and will make it desolate forever...'"

The prophecy was written between 626-586 BC, and it was fulfilled in the 609 BC to 539 BC time period. The prophet said that Jews would suffer 70 years of Babylonian domination. Jeremiah also said Babylon would be punished after 70 years. Both parts of this prophecy were fulfilled.

In 609 BC, Babylon took many Jews as captives to Babylon, destroying Jerusalem and the Temple. 70 yrs later, the domination ended in 539 BC, when Cyrus, a leader of Persians and Medes, conquered Babylon and brought an end to its empire. Cyrus later offered the captive Jews the freedom to return to their homeland.

B. Babylon's gates would open for Cyrus.

Isaiah 45:1 says, "This is what the Lord says to his anointed, to Cyrus, whose right hand I take hold of to subdue nations before him and to strip kings of their armor, to open doors before him so that gates will not be shut…"

The prophecy was written between 701-681 BC, and it was fulfilled in 539 BC. Despite Babylon's remarkable defenses, which included moats and walls that were more than 70 feet thick and 300 feet high with 250 watchtowers, Cyrus was able to enter the city and conquer it.

C. Babylon's kingdom would be permanently overthrown.

The Bible prophesied this in Isaiah 13:19: "Babylon, the jewel of kingdoms, the glory of the Babylonians' pride, will be overthrown by God like Sodom and Gomorrah."

The prophecy was written between 701-681 BC and it was fulfilled in 539 BC. The prophet said Babylon would be overthrown, permanently. History confirms it when Cyrus conquered Babylon in 539 BC; it never again rose to power as an empire.

D. Babylon would be reduced to swampland.

So says Isaiah 14:23: "'I will turn her into a place for owls and into swampland; I will sweep her with the broom of destruction,' declares the Lord Almighty."

The prophecy was written between 701-681 BC, and it was fulfilled in 539 BC. The prophet said that Babylon, which had been a world power at two different times in history, would be brought to a humble and final end. It would be reduced to swampland. After Cyrus conquered Babylon in 539 BC, the kingdom never again rose to power. The buildings of Babylon fell into a gradual state of ruin during the next several centuries. Archaeologists excavated Babylon during the 1800s. Some parts of the city could not be dug up because they were under a water table that had risen over the years.

Babylon was one of the greatest cities of ancient times. Its hanging gardens were one of the seven wonders of the world. Babylon was surrounded by walls 14 miles long, 187 feet thick, and 200 feet high, and its towers extended another 100 feet above the walls. Yet, God said in Jeremiah 51:58-62: "Babylon's thick wall will be leveled and her high gates set on fire..." Both Isaiah and Jeremiah predicted that Babylon would never be inhabited again (Jeremiah 50:39).

When Alexander the Great issued orders to rebuild Babylon, he was struck dead within a week, and his project was abandoned. In 1983, when Iraqi president Saddam Hussein started rebuilding Babylon on top of the ancient ruins, he inscribed his name on many of the bricks in imitation of Nebuchadnezzar. One frequent inscription reads: "This was built by Saddam Hussein, son of Nebuchadnezzar, to glorify Iraq." On November 5, 2006, Hussein was found guilty of crimes against humanity by the Iraqi Special Tribunal. He was executed for these crimes on December 30, 2006.

After the downfall of Hussein, the inscribed bricks from Babylon became sought after as collector's items, and the ruins of Babylon are no longer being restored to their original state.

Statistics

Our fourth MAPS principle aligns with predictive prophecy because it is statistically preposterous that any or all of the Bible's very specific detailed prophecies could have been fulfilled through chance, good guessing, or deliberate deceit!

Mathematician Peter Stoner, former chair of the Department of Mathematics and Astronomy at Pasadena City College and chair of the Science Division at Westmont College, calculated the mathematical probability of the specific fulfillment of numerous prophetic predictions in the Bible.

According to Stoner, the probability of the predictions concerning Tyre is one in 7.5×10^7. The probability of the fulfillment of the Babylonian predictions by Isaiah of Jerusalem and Jeremiah according to Stoner is 1 in 5×10^9.

No one has ever prophesied in their writings that a human being would rise from the dead and ascend into heaven. Why? Because the chances of it happening by coincidence is incalculable, and when it does *not* happen, that person is proven a false prophet. Yet, in the Scripture, there are well over 300 prophecies in the Old Testament about the coming Messiah, and Jesus fulfills them all!

Fulfilled Prophecy: Evidence for the Reliability of the Bible

Unique among all books ever written, the Bible accurately foretells specific events in detail many years, sometimes centuries, before they occur. Approximately 2,500 prophecies appear in the pages of the Bible, about 2,000 of which already have been fulfilled to the letter—no errors. The remaining 500 or so reach into the future and may be seen unfolding as days go by.

Since the probability for any one of these prophecies having been fulfilled by chance averages less than one in ten (figured very conservatively) and since the prophecies are for the most part independent of one another, the odds for all these prophecies having been fulfilled by chance without error is less than one in 10^{2000}—that is 1 with 2,000 zeros written after it!

The test for identifying a prophet of God is recorded by Moses in Deuteronomy 18:21-22. According to this Bible passage (and others), God's prophets, as distinct from Satan's spokesmen (false prophets), are 100 percent accurate in their predictions. There is *no* room for error.

The Statistics Themselves

(1) Some time before 500 BC, the prophet Daniel proclaimed that Israel's long-awaited Messiah would begin his public ministry 483 years after the issuing of a decree to restore and rebuild Jerusalem (Daniel 9:25-26). He further predicted that the Messiah would be "cut off," killed, and that this event would take place prior to a second destruction of Jerusalem.

Abundant documentation shows that these prophecies were perfectly fulfilled in the life (and crucifixion) of Jesus Christ. The decree regarding the restoration of Jerusalem was issued by Persia's King Artaxerxes to the Hebrew priest Ezra in 458 BC, 483 years later the ministry of Jesus Christ began in Galilee. Remember that, due to calendar changes, the date for the start of Christ's ministry is set by most historians at about AD 26. Also note that from 1 BC to AD 1 is just one year, not two. Jesus' crucifixion occurred only a few years later, and about four decades later, in AD 70, came the destruction of Jerusalem by Titus.

Probability of chance fulfillment = 1 in 10^5

(2) In approximately 700 BC, the prophet Micah named the tiny village of Bethlehem as the birthplace of Israel's Messiah (Micah 5:2). The fulfillment of this prophecy in the birth of Christ is one of the most widely known and widely celebrated facts in history.

Probability of chance fulfillment = 1 in 10^5

(3) In the fifth century BC, a prophet named Zechariah declared that the Messiah would be betrayed for the price of a slave—thirty pieces of silver, according to Jewish law—and also that this money would be used to buy a burial ground for Jerusalem's poor foreigners (Zechariah 11:12-13). Bible writers and secular historians both record thirty pieces of silver as the sum paid to Judas Iscariot for betraying Jesus, and they indicate that the money went to purchase a "potter's field," used—just as predicted—for the burial of poor aliens (Matthew 27:3-10).

Probability of chance fulfillment = 1 in 10^{11}

(4) Some 400 years before crucifixion was invented, both Israel's King David and the prophet Zechariah described the Messiah's death in words that perfectly depict that mode of execution. Further, they said that the body would be pierced and that none of the bones would be broken, contrary to customary procedure in cases of crucifixion (Psalm 22 and 34:20; Zechariah 12:10).

Again, historians and New Testament writers confirm the fulfillment: Jesus of Nazareth died on a Roman cross, and his extraordinarily quick death eliminated the need for the usual breaking of bones. A spear was thrust into his side to verify that he was, indeed, dead.

Probability of chance fulfillment = 1 in 10^{13}

(5) The prophet Isaiah foretold that a conqueror named Cyrus would destroy seemingly impregnable Babylon and subdue Egypt along with most of the rest of the known world. This same man, said Isaiah, would decide to let the Jewish exiles in his territory go free without any payment of ransom (Isaiah 44:28; 45:1; and 45:13). Isaiah made this prophecy 150 years before Cyrus was born, 180 years before Cyrus performed any of these feats (and he did, eventually, perform them all), and 80 years before the Jews were taken into exile.

Probability of chance fulfillment = 1 in 10^{15}

(6) Mighty Babylon, 196 miles square, was enclosed not only by a moat, but also by a double wall 330 feet high, each part 90 feet thick. It was said by unanimous popular opinion to be indestructible, yet two Bible prophets declared its doom. These prophets further claimed that the ruins would be avoided by travelers, that the city would never again be inhabited, and that its stones would not even be moved for use as building material (Isaiah 13:17-22 and Jeremiah 51:26, 43). Their description is, in fact, the well-documented history of the famous citadel.

Probability of chance fulfillment = 1 in 10^9

(7) The exact location and construction sequence of Jerusalem's nine suburbs was predicted by Jeremiah about 2600 years ago. He referred to the time of this building project as "the last days," that is, the time period of Israel's second rebirth as a nation in the land of Palestine (Jeremiah 31:38-40). This rebirth became history in 1948, and the construction of the nine suburbs has gone forward precisely in the locations and in the sequence predicted.

Probability of chance fulfillment = 1 in 10^{18}

(8) The prophet Moses foretold (with some additions by Jeremiah and Jesus) that the ancient Jewish nation would be conquered twice and that the people would be carried off as slaves each time, first by the Babylonians, for a period of 70 years, and then by a fourth world kingdom, which we know as Rome. The second conqueror, Moses said, would take the Jews captive to Egypt in ships, selling them or giving them away as slaves to all parts of the world. Both of these predictions were fulfilled to the letter, the first in 607 BC and the second in AD 70. God's spokesman said that Jews would remain scattered throughout the entire world for many generations, but without becoming assimilated by the peoples or of other nations, and that the Jews would one day return to the land of Palestine to re-establish for a second time their nation (Deuteronomy 29; Isaiah 11:11-13; Jeremiah 25:11; Hosea 3:4-5; and Luke 21:23-24).

This prophetic statement sweeps across 3,500 years of history to its complete fulfillment—in our lifetime.

Probability of chance fulfillment = 1 in 10^{20}

(9) Jeremiah predicted that despite its fertility and despite the accessibility of its water supply, the land of Edom (today a part of Jordan) would become a barren, uninhabited wasteland (Jeremiah 49:15-20; Ezekiel 25:12-14). His description accurately tells the history of that now bleak region.

Probability of chance fulfillment = 1 in 10^{5}

(10) Joshua prophesied that Jericho would be rebuilt by one man. He also said that the man's eldest son would die when the reconstruction began and that his youngest son would die when the work reached completion (Joshua 6:26). About five centuries later this prophecy found its fulfillment in the life and family of a man named Hiel (1 Kings 16:33-34).

Probability of chance fulfillment = 1 in 10^{7}

(11) The day of Elijah's supernatural departure from Earth was predicted unanimously—and accurately, according to the eye-witness account—by a group of fifty prophets (2 Kings 2:3-11).

Probability of chance fulfillment = 1 in 10^{9}

(12) Jahaziel prophesied that King Jehoshaphat and a tiny band of men would defeat an enormous, well-equipped, well-trained army without even having to fight. Just as predicted, the King and his troops stood looking on as their foes were supernaturally destroyed to the last man (2 Chronicles 20).

Probability of chance fulfillment = 1 in 10^{8}

(13) One prophet of God (unnamed, but probably Shemiah) said that a future king of Judah, named Josiah, would take the bones of all the occultic priests (priests of the "high places") of Israel's King Jeroboam and burn them on Jeroboam's altar (1 Kings 13:2 and 2 Kings 23:15-18). This event occurred approximately 300 years after it was foretold.

Probability of chance fulfillment = 1 in 10^{13}

The estimates of probability included herein come from a group of secular research scientists. As an example of their method of estimation, consider their calculations for this first prophecy cited:

- ✦ Since the Messiah's ministry could conceivably begin in any 1 of about 5000 years, there is, then, 1 chance in about 5,000 that his ministry could begin in AD 26.

- ✦ Since the Messiah is God in human form, the possibility of his being killed is considerably low, say less than 1 chance in 10.

- ✦ Relative to the second destruction of Jerusalem, this execution has roughly an even chance of occurring before or after that event, that is, 1 chance in 2.

- ✦ Hence, the probability of chance fulfillment for this prophecy is 1 in 5,000 x 10 x 2, which is 1 in 100,000, or 1 in 10^5.

Since these thirteen prophecies cover mostly separate and independent events, the probability of chance occurrence for all thirteen is about 1 in 10^{138} (138 equals the sum of all the exponents of 10 in the probability estimates above).

For the sake of putting the figure into perspective, this probability can be compared to the statistical chance that the second law of thermodynamics will be reversed in a given situation. For example, that a gasoline engine will refrigerate itself during its combustion cycle or that heat will flow from a cold body to a hot body—that chance is equal to 1 in 10^{80}.

Stating it simply, based on these thirteen prophecies alone, the Bible record may be said to be vastly more reliable than the second law of thermodynamics. Each reader should feel free to make his own reasonable estimates of probability for the chance fulfillment of the prophecies cited here. In any case, the probabilities deduced still will be absurdly remote.

Given that the Bible proves so reliable a document, there is every reason to expect that the remaining 500 prophecies, those slated for the "time of the end," also will be fulfilled to the last letter. Who can afford to ignore these coming events, much less miss out on the immeasurable blessings offered to anyone and everyone who submits to the control of the Bible's author, Jesus Christ? Would a reasonable person take lightly God's warning of judgment for those who reject what they know to be true about Jesus Christ and the Bible, or who reject Jesus' claim on their lives?

The Bible comments on a belief system which promises the practitioner peace and a better life. From Confucius to Ron Hubbard, myriads of books set forth similar claims. So what sets the Bible apart from this mountain of literature different from the rest?

One aspect differentiating the Bible from other religious, historical or inspirational works is this: throughout the Bible, future events are predicted with verifiable accuracy. If the Bible predicted the future (what biblical writers call prophecy) to the extent that it cannot be dismissed as mere coincidence, then the source of this book can only be an omnipotent, omnipresent, omniscient Godwhochosetospeakhiswordthroughindividualsforhispurposesanddesign. Let's consider the evidence.

The more you investigate the historical record within the Bible, the more you can find events such as these. Occurring repeatedly, the only way for writers to accurately predict the future is with the input of the One outside these space time events.

At the Bible's epicenter is Jesus Christ, who fulfills more prophetic proclamations than any other person. During his lifetime, Jesus fulfilled close to 300 prophetic forecasts, many of which were written hundreds of years before his birth. Mathematically, this is a statistical impossibility. The odds of Jesus completing these prophetic promises during his lifetime are the same as successfully completing the following task.

Do other religious works include the same prophetic content? The answer is no. The writings from the Far East, the teachings of Confucius, Buddhism, and Hinduism do not even make a claim to be God's word. They present to their followers a path to a simpler, more satisfactory life. The Quran makes no claims to being words from Allah. Rather it is the writing of Mohammed, a religious leader, his record of what Allah told him, paired with history. But has any prophecy in the Quran come to pass? Only the Christian Bible claims to be God's very word to man and only the Bible contains the verifiable track record of prophetic fulfillment as evidence of its claims. No other religious group or religious writings can make the same claim.

When you look at some of the improbable prophecies of the Old and New Testaments, it seems incredible that skeptics knowing the authenticity and historicity of the texts could reject the verdict: the Bible is the Word of God and Jesus Christ is the Son of God, just as Scripture predicted many times and in many ways.

OLD TESTAMENT PROPHECIES FULFILLED BY JESUS

Born a Virgin

+ Isaiah 7:14: "Therefore the Lord Himself will give you a sign: The virgin will conceive and give birth to a son, and will call Him Immanuel."

+ Matthew 1:20-23, "[20]But after he had considered this, an angel of the Lord appeared to him in a dream and said, 'Joseph son of David, do not be afraid to take Mary home as your wife, because what is conceived in her is from the Holy Spirit. [21] She will give birth to a son, and you are to give Him the name Jesus, because He will save His people from their sins.' [22] All this took place to fulfill what the Lord had said through the prophet: [23] 'The virgin will be with child and will give birth to a son, and they will call Him Immanuel (which means, 'God with us.')"

Descended from Abraham, David

+ Genesis 12:3, "I will bless those who bless you, and whoever curses you I will curse; and all peoples on earth will be blessed through you."

+ Isaiah 16:5, "In love a throne will be established; in faithfulness a man will sit on it—one from the house of David—one who in judging seeks justice and speeds the cause of righteousness."

+ Matthew 1:1, "This is the genealogy of Jesus the Messiah, the son of David, the son of Abraham."

Born in Bethlehem

+ Micah 5:2, "But you, Bethlehem Ephrathah, though you are small among the clans of Judah, out of you will come for me one who will be ruler over Israel, whose origins are from of old, from ancient times."

- ✦ Matthew 2:1, "After Jesus was born in Bethlehem in Judea, during the time of King Herod, (A caste of wise men specializing in astronomy, astrology, and natural science) magi from the east arrived in Jerusalem."

His Birth Would Trigger a Massacre of Infant Boys

- ✦ Jeremiah 31:15, "This is what the LORD says: 'A voice is heard in Ramah, mourning and great weeping, Rachel is weeping for her children and refusing to be comforted because they are no more.'"

- ✦ Matthew 2:16, "When Herod realized that he had been outwitted by the magi, he was furious, and he gave orders to kill all the boys in Bethlehem and its vicinity who were two years old and under, in accordance with the time he had learned from the magi."

Ministry Would Include Miraculous Healings

- ✦ Isaiah 29:18, "In that day the deaf will hear the words of the scroll, and out of gloom and darkness the eyes of the blind will see."

- ✦ Luke 7:21, "At that very time Jesus cured many who had diseases, sicknesses and evil spirits, and gave sight to many who were blind."

Jesus Would Claim to Be God

- ✦ Isaiah 9:6, "For to us a child is born, to us a son is given, and the government will be on His shoulders; And He will be called Wonderful Counselor, Mighty God, Everlasting Father, Prince of Peace."

- ✦ John 10:30, "I and the Father are one."

Entered Jerusalem on a Donkey

✦ Zechariah 9:9, "Rejoice greatly, Daughter Zion! Shout, Daughter of Jerusalem! See, your king comes to you, righteous and victorious, lowly and riding on a donkey, on a colt, the foal of a donkey."

✦ Matthew 21:4-9 [This quotes the prophecy in Zech 9:9], "The disciples went and did as Jesus had instructed them. They brought the donkey and the colt and placed their cloaks on them for Jesus to sit on. A very large crowd spread their cloaks on the road, while others cut branches from the trees and spread them on the road. The crowds that went ahead of Him and those that followed shouted, 'Hosanna to the Son of David!'"

Betrayed By a Friend

✦ Psalms 41:9, "Even my close friend, someone I trusted, one who shared my bread, has turned against me."

✦ Matthew 26:47-50, "While He was still speaking, Judas, one of the Twelve, arrived. With him was a large crowd armed with swords and clubs, sent from the chief priests and the elders of the people. Now the betrayer had arranged a signal with them: 'The one I kiss is the man; arrest Him.' Going at once to Jesus, Judas said, 'Greetings, Rabbi!' and kissed Him. Jesus replied, 'Do what you came for, friend.' Then the men stepped forward, seized Jesus and arrested Him."

Betrayed for 30 Pieces of Silver

✦ Zechariah 11:12, "I told them, 'If you think it best, give me my pay; but if not, keep it.' So they paid me thirty pieces of silver."

✦ Matthew 26:14-15, "Then one of the Twelve—the one called Judas Iscariot— went to the chief priests and asked, 'What are you willing to give me if I deliver him over to you?' So they counted out for him thirty silver coins."

Disciples Would Scatter

+ Zechariah 13:7, "'Awake, sword, against my shepherd, against the man who is close to me!' declares the LORD Almighty. 'Strike the shepherd, and the sheep will be scattered, and I will turn my hand against the little ones.'"

+ Matthew 26:31, "Then Jesus told them, 'This very night you will all fall away on account of me, for it is written: I will strike the shepherd, and the sheep of the flock will be scattered.'"

Crucified with Other Criminals

+ Isaiah 53:12, "Therefore, I will give Him a portion among the great, and He will divide the spoils with the strong, because He poured out His life unto death, and was numbered with the transgressors. For He bore the sin of many, and made intercession for the transgressors."

+ Luke 23:32-33, "Two other men, both criminals, were also led out with Him to be executed. When they came to the place called the Skull, they crucified Him there, along with the criminals— one on His right and the other on His left."

Crucified, Pierced in the Hands and Feet

+ Psalm 22:16, "Dogs surround Me, a pack of villains encircles Me; they pierce My hands and My feet."

+ John 20:27, "Then He said to Thomas, Put your finger here; see My hands. Reach out your hand and put it into My side. Stop doubting and believe.

Clothes were Divided Up By Lots

+ Psalm 22:18, "They divide My clothes among them and cast lots for My garments."

+ Matthew 27:35, "When they had crucified Him, they divided up His garments among themselves by casting lots."

None of His Bones were Broken

+ Psalm 34:20, "He protects all his bones, not one of them will be broken."

+ John 19:33, "But when they came to Jesus and found that He was already dead, they did not break His legs."

His Burial Among the Rich

+ Isaiah 53:9, "He was assigned a grave with the wicked, and with the rich in death, though He had done no violence, nor was any deceit in His mouth."

+ Matthew 27:57-60, "As evening approached, there came a rich man from Arimathea, named Joseph, who had himself become a disciple of Jesus. Going to Pilate, he asked for Jesus' body, and Pilate ordered that it be given to him. Joseph took the body, wrapped it in a clean linen cloth, and placed it in his own new tomb and went away."

Silver Returned, Then Used to Buy Potter's Field

+ Zechariah 11:12, "I told them, 'If you think it best, give me my pay; but if not, keep it.' So they paid me thirty pieces of silver."

+ Matthew 27:3-7, "When Judas, who had betrayed Him, saw that Jesus was condemned, he was seized with remorse and returned the thirty pieces of silver to the chief priests and the elders. 'I have sinned,' he said, "for I have betrayed innocent blood.' 'What is that to us?' they replied.' 'That's your responsibility.' So Judas threw the money into the temple and left. Then he went away and hanged himself. The chief priests picked up the coins and said, 'It is against the law to put this into the treasury, since it is blood money.' So they decided to use the money to buy the potter's field as a burial place for foreigners."

Jesus Would Die, and Then Rise on the Third Day

✦ Psalms 16:10, "Because you will not abandon me to the realm of the dead, nor will you let your faithful one see decay."

✦ Mark 8:31, "He then began to teach them that the Son of Man must suffer many things and be rejected by the elders, the chief priests and the teachers of the law, and that he must be killed and after three days rise again."

✦ Matthew 28:1, "After the Sabbath, at dawn on the first day of the week, Mary Magdalene and the other Mary went to look at the tomb."

Two Tests of a True Prophet

1. "But a prophet who presumes to speak in my name anything I have not commanded, or a prophet who speaks in the name of other gods, is to be put to death.' 'But you say to yourselves, 'How can we know when a message has not been spoken by the Lord?' If what a prophet proclaims in the name of the Lord does not take place or come true, that is a message the Lord has not spoken. That prophet has spoken presumptuously, so do not be alarmed'" (Deuteronomy 18:20-22).

2. "If a prophet, or one who foretells by dreams, appears among you and announces to you a sign or wonder, and if the sign or wonder spoken of takes place, and the prophet says, 'Let us follow other gods' (gods you have not known) 'and let us worship them,' you must not listen to the words of that prophet or dreamer. The Lord your God is testing you to find out whether you love Him with all your heart and with all your soul. It is the Lord your God you must follow, and Him you must revere. Keep his commands and obey Him; serve Him and hold fast to Him. That prophet or dreamer must be put to death for inciting rebellion against the Lord your God, who brought you out of Egypt and redeemed you from the land of slavery. That prophet or dreamer tried to turn you from the way the Lord your God commanded you to follow. You must purge the evil from among you" (Deuteronomy 13:1-5).

First, you must test the prophecy, and second, you must test the teaching. Are these prophets leading you to the worship of the true and living God, or are they leading you to false gods and teaching contrary to God's Word? *Even if the prophecy comes true, you must test the teaching by the Word of God.*

"But even if we or an angel from heaven *should preach a gospel* other than the one we preached to you, *let them be under God's curse!* As we have already said, so now I say again: If anybody is preaching to you a gospel other than what you accepted, let them be under God's curse!" (Galatians 1:8-9)

Islam states that Jesus wasn't the last prophet but instead points to Muhammed. Mohammad claimed angel Gabriel came to him and that he received revelations during which he would go into epileptic fits. These revelations were written down into what is now the Quran. These revelations said there is no god but Allah.

Man is God's slave and his first duty is to submit—"Islam" means submission—that he was to loot and steal from caravans passing through and then kill the men and Islam was to be exalted above all other religions.

The Abrahamic Faiths

The primary difference among the three Abrahamic faiths is over the **divinity of Jesus**. Jews and Muslims reject the triune conception of God and place primacy on belief in One God. Christians, on the other hand, contend that Jesus was the incarnate son of God who sacrificed his life for the salvation of others. Muslims believe that salvation is to be achieved by the belief in One God and performing righteous deeds seeking to please God.

Jesus proved His authority and divinity by His resurrection! (John 2:18-20)

What Islam Teaches About Jesus

Muslims accept that Jesus was a servant, teacher, and lover of God's Word, though they do not believe that he was divine or the son of God. The Quran describes the miracles Jesus performed, such as healing the sick and raising the dead, but does not ascribe these miracles to his divinity. Instead, Jesus is a sign of God's endless mercy to all humankind.

Muslims believe that Jesus was a prophet who was given a special message—*injil*, or the gospel—to convey to all people. This message both confirmed what was taught in the Torah and foretold the coming of Prophet Muhammad. Thus, Jesus has a vital and unique role to play in the Muslim faith.

Muslims do not believe in original sin. They see no need for a savior and, moreover, do not believe in Jesus' crucifixion. The Quran states that Jesus was assumed into heaven before his actual death. Islamic tradition explains that Jesus was spared death because he was God's holy one.

"In the past God spoke to our ancestors through the prophets at many times and in various ways, but in these last days He has spoken to us by His Son, whom He appointed heir of all things, and through whom also He made the universe" (Hebrews 1:1-2).

"Jesus answered, 'I am the way and the truth and the life. No one comes to the Father except through Me'" (John 14:6).

"Two men, Moses and Elijah, appeared in glorious splendor, talking with Jesus.....A voice came from the cloud, saying, 'This is My Son, whom I have chosen; listen to Him'" (Luke 9:30; 9:35).

"Salvation is found in no one else, for there is no other name under heaven given to mankind by which we must be saved" (Acts 4:12).

Conclusion of Apologetics

The next time someone denies the reliability of Scripture, just remember the acronym MAPS, and you will be equipped to give an answer and reason for the hope that lies within you (1 Peter 3:15). Manuscripts, Archaeology, Prophecy, and Statistics not only chart a secure course on the turnpikes of skepticism, but also definitively demonstrate that the Bible is indeed divine rather than human in origin.

Jesus is unique among all people in history in that He is the fulfillment of centuries of Messianic prophecies, which are found in the Old Testament of the Bible; these foretold his place of birth, details of his life, his mission, his nature, his death, and his resurrection.

"Jesus said to them, 'This is what I told you while I was still with you: Everything must be fulfilled that is written about me in the Law of Moses, the Prophets and the Psalms'" (Luke 24:44).

Need more resources? Check out IMG's website to view our recommendations, most notably the four pamphlets by Rose Publishing over:

✦ Christianity, Cults & Religions

✦ Denominations Comparison: Compare 12 Major Denominations and Their Beliefs

✦ Essential Doctrine Made Easy: Key Christian Beliefs

✦ Why Trust the Bible?

There are so many additional resources available in this area:

✦ Dr. Kent Hovind (Dr. Dino)

✦ Ken Ham (Answers in Genesis)

✦ Lee Strobel (The Case for Christ)

✦ Josh McDowell, (Evidence That Demands a Verdict)

✦ Norman Geisler and Frank Turek (I Don't Have Enough Faith to Be an Atheist)

Our favorite resources are:

- ✦ The Truth Project by Dr. Del Tackett

- ✦ Impact 360 Institute

- ✦ Biblical-e-learning.org

- ✦ Stand to Reason

- ✦ Inspiring Philosophy

- ✦ Dr. Craig Videos (Reasonable Faith)

- ✦ The Gospel Coalition (One Minute Apologetics)

- ✦ J. Warner Wallace (Cold Case Christianity).

We also like video content by: Brad Gray, Allen Parr, Jobi Martin, Bible Project. This is just some of what is out there.

REFERENCES

Chapter One

Buice, Josh. "Lost Church Members." G3 Ministries. May 21, 2015. https://g3min. org/lost-church-members/.

Nails, Wayne. "My How The Church Has Declined." Walk With God. Accessed September 12, 2022. http://walkwithgodthejourney.com/thoughts/my-how-the-church-has-declined-4/.

Newport, Frank. "Percentage of Christians in U.S. Drifting Down, but Still High." *Gallup*. December 24, 2015. https://news.gallup.com/poll/187955/percentage-christians-drifting-down-high.aspx.

Smith, Gregory A. "About Three-in-Ten U.S. Adults Are Now Religiously Unaffiliated." Pew Research. December 14, 2021. https://www.pewresearch. org/religion/2021/12/14/about-three-in-ten-u-s-adults-are-now-religiously-unaffiliated/.

Gecewicz, Claire, and Gregory A. Smith. "White Evangelicals See Trump as Fighting for Their Beliefs, Though Many Have Mixed Feelings About His Personal Conduct." Pew Research. March 12, 2020. https://www. pewresearch.org/religion/2020/03/12/views-about-religion-in-american-society/.

"51% of Churchgoers Don't Know of the Great Commission." Barna. March 27, 2018. https://www.barna.com/research/half-churchgoers-not-heard-great-commission/.

Alper, Becka A., and Gregory A. Smith. "What Americans Know About Religion." Pew Research. July 23, 2019. https://www.pewresearch.org/religion/2019/07/23/what-americans-know-about-religion/.

Smith, Gregory A. "About Three-in-Ten U.S. Adults Are Now Religiously Unaffiliated." Pew Research. December 14, 2021. https://www.pewresearch.org/religion/2021/12/14/about-three-in-ten-u-s-adults-are-now-religiously-unaffiliated/.

"The Relationship Between Volunteering and Giving." Barna. August 21, 2018. https://www.barna.com/research/volunteering-giving/.

"What Motivates Christians to Give?" Barna. November 27, 2018. https://www.barna.com/research/motivations-for-generosity/.

"New Study Shows Trends in Tithing and Donating." Barna. April 14, 2008. https://www.barna.com/research/new-study-shows-trends-in-tithing-and-donating/.

"Generations & Generosity: How Age Affects Giving." Barna. September 26, 2017. https://www.barna.com/research/generations-generosity-age-affects-giving/

"What People Experience in Churches." Barna. January 8, 2012. https://www.barna.com/research/what-people-experience-in-churches/.

"Surveys Show Pastors Claim Congregants Are Deeply Committed to God But Congregants Deny It!" Barna. January 10, 2006. https://www.barna.com/research/surveys-show-pastors-claim-congregants-are-deeply-committed-to-god-but-congregants-deny-it/.

"Two in Five Christians Are Not Engaged in Discipleship." Barna. January 26, 2022. https://www.barna.com/research/christians-discipleship-community/.

"1 in 4 Practicing Christians Struggles To Forgive Someone." Barna. April 11, 2019. https://www.barna.com/research/forgiveness-christians/.

Chapter Two

"Apologetics." Britannica. September 6, 2022. https://www.britannica.com/topic/apologetics.

"Group Leader Resources." Real Life. Accessed September 12, 2022. https://real.life/group-resources/.

Chapter Three

Smith, Matthew. "World War II and Mental Health." *Psychology Today*. November 17, 2020. https://www.psychologytoday.com/us/blog/short-history-mental-health/202011/world-war-ii-and-mental-health.

"Spirit, Soul and Body—How God Designed Us." Faith and Health Connection. Accessed September 13, 2022. https://www.faithandhealthconnection.org/the_connection/spirit-soul-and-body/.

"Discover Your Leadership Style." Association of Related Church. Accessed September 13, 2022. https://www.arcchurches.com/disc/.

Chapter Five

Zak, Heidi. "Adults Make More Than 35,000 Decisions Per Day. Here Are 4 Ways to Prevent Mental Burnout." *Inc.* https://www.inc.com/heidi-zak/adults-make-more-than-35000-decisions-per-day-here-are-4-ways-to-prevent-mental-burnout.html.

Appendix

Smith, Gary W. *Life Changing Thoughts*. Bloomington, IN: AuthorHouse, 2009.

Kragh, Helge. "What's in a Name: History and Meanings of the Term 'Big Bang.'" *ArXiv: History and Philosophy of Physics* (2013): 1-47. https://doi.org/10.48550/arXiv.1301.0219.

Rolston III, Holmes. "Shaken Atheism: A Look at the Fine-Tuned Universe." Religion Online. Accessed September 13, 2022. https://www.religion-online.org/article/shaken-atheism-a-look-at-the-fine-tuned-universe/.

Hawking, Stephen, and Roger Penrose. *The Nature of Space and Time.* Princeton: Princeton University Press, 1996.

Shahmordian, Feridoun Shawn. *Reign of the Essence: Encyclopedia of Critical Thinking.* Bloomington, IN: Authorhouse, 2022.

Ball, Steven. "A Christian Physicist Examines the Big Bang Theory." LeTourneau University. September 13, 2022. https://www.letu.edu/academics/arts-and-sciences/files/big-bang.pdf.

Dawkins, Richard, and Yan Wong. *The Ancestor's Tale: A Pilgrimage to the Dawn of Evolution.* New York: Mariner Books, 2016.

Hawking, Stephen, and Leonard Mlodinow. *The Grand Design.* New York: Bantam Books, 2010.

"Anthropic University." Oregon University. Accessed September 13, 2022. http://abyss.uoregon.edu/~js/cosmo/lectures/lec24.html.

Hawking, Stephen. *A Brief History of Time.* New York: Bantam Books, 1998.

Dyson, Freeman. *Disturbing the Universe.* New York: Basic Books, 1981.

Davies, Paul. *The Cosmic Blueprint: New Discoveries in Nature's Creative Ability to Order the Universe.* West Conshohocken, PA: Templeton Foundation Press, 2007.

"Cosmological Scale." Collins Dictionary. Accessed September 13, 2022. https://www.collinsdictionary.com/us/dictionary/english/cosmological-scale.

"Cosmetic." Collins Dictionary. Accessed September 13, 2022. https://www.collinsdictionary.com/us/dictionary/english/cosmetic.

Comfort, Ray, and Robert S. Cameron. *School Of Biblical Evangelism: 101 Lessons: How To Share Your Faith Simply, Effectively, Biblically... The Way Jesus Did.* Gainesville, FL: Bridge-Logos Publishers, 2018.

Moore, Frazier. "The Universe made simple by an extraordinary mind." *Tampa Bay Times*. October 12, 1997. https://www.tampabay.com/archive/1997/10/12/the-universe-made-simple-by-an-extraordinary-mind/#:~:text=%22Yet%2C%20in%20another,and%20so%20on%20.

Paulson, Steve. "The Believer." Salon. August 7, 2006. https://www.salon.com/2006/08/07/collins_6/.

Feynman, Richard P. *The Meaning of It All: Thoughts of a Citizen-Scientist*. Reading, MA: Addison-Wesley, 1998.

Thompson, Dietrick E. "The Quantum Universe: A Zero-Point Fluctuation?" *Science News*. August 3, 1985. https://www.sciencenews.org/archive/quantum-universe-zero-point-fluctuation.

Drake, Nadia. "What is the Multiverse—And is There Any Evidence It Really Exists?" *National Geographic*. May 4, 2022. https://www.nationalgeographic.com/science/article/what-is-the-multiverse.

Scoles, Sarah. "Can Physicists Ever Prove the Multiverse Is Real?" *Smithsonian Magazine*. April 19, 2016. https://www.smithsonianmag.com/science-nature/can-physicists-ever-prove-multiverse-real-180958813/.

Garrett, Gregory Lessing. *No Apology Necessary Atheism Refuted: Eternal Causal Intelligence Affirmed A Comprehensive Compendium of Intelligent Refutations to Atheism*. Hollister, CA: Lulu Publishing, 2018.

"Evolutionary Trinity." Grace To You. Accessed September 13, 2022. https://www.gty.org/library/Print/Blog/B100502.

Dawkins, Richard. *The Blind Watchmaker: Why the Evidence of Evolution Reveals a Universe Without Design*. New York: W. W. Norton & Company, 2015.

Truman, Royal. "Information Theory—Part 2: Weaknesses in Current Conceptual Frameworks." *Journal of Creation* 26, no. 3 (2012): 107-114. https://creation.com/images/pdfs/tj/j26_3/j26_3_107-114.pdf.

Ham, Ken, and Jason Lisle. "Is There Really a God?" Answers in Genesis. August 9, 2007. https://answersingenesis.org/is-god-real/is-there-really-god/.

"Best-selling Book." Guinness World Records. 2021. https://www.guinnessworldrecords.com/world-records/best-selling-book-of-non-fiction.

Hanegraaff, Hank. *Has God Spoken?: Memorable Proof of the Bible's Divine Inspiration*. 3rd ed. Nashville: Thomas Nelson, 2011.

Chernow, Barbara A., and George A. Vallaski, eds. *The Columbia Encyclopedia*. 5th ed. Columbia: Columbia University Press, 1993.

Ross, Hugh. "Fulfilled Prophecy: Evidence for the Reliability of the Bible." Reasons. August 22, 2003. https://reasons.org/explore/publications/articles/fulfilled-prophecy-evidence-for-the-reliability-of-the-bible.

Burns, Tim. "Why is the Bible, and Not Other Religious Books, the Word of God?" CBN. Accessed September 13, 2022. https://www1.cbn.com/spirituallife/the-word-of-god.

"100prophecies.org." Accessed September 13, 2022. https://www.100prophecies.org/.

ABOUT THE AUTHOR

Chris Wasman is the co-founder and CEO of Istoria Ministry Group (IMG), a Christ-centered nonprofit that pours all of their resources into helping others enhance their stories by challenging them to go beyond "surface-level" in their faith journey. Chris' story, like so many others, is one of hurts, brokenness, and mistakes, but it also includes redemption and restoration with God's signature all over it, suiting him to link arms with others as they seek to experience more in their faith.

Prior to IMG, Chris spent more than ten years serving in various high-impact roles within some of the fastest growing churches in the nation, leveraging his passion for people to lead several different ministries.

In his early years, Chris served with the United States Marines in Desert Storm and earned multiple service awards during that time. He spent a large part of his professional career in the fast-paced world of online travel with leading Fortune 500 brands. Holding roles which ranged from market-level to executive management, Chris has had the opportunity to learn and lead at every level.

Chris earned a Bachelor of Science degree in Psychology from the University of Central Florida, a Master of Arts degree in Pastoral Counseling from Liberty University, and is currently acquiring dual certifications as a Christian Life Coach (CCLC) and Professional Life Coach (CPLC).

Made in the USA
Las Vegas, NV
06 October 2022

56645882R00098